Why Jesus didn't
Mary Magdalene

Why Jesus didn't marry Mary Magdalene

John van Schaik

Floris Books

Translated by George Hall

First published in Dutch in 2006
under the title *Waarom Jezus niet
getrouwd was met Maria Magdalena*
by Uitgeverij Christofoor, Zeist
First published in English in 2007
by Floris Books, Edinburgh

British Library CIP Data available

ISBN 978-086315-582-6

Printed by Cromwell Press, Trowbridge

Contents

Foreword

Another book on *The Da Vinci Code?* So much has been written on this subject already. However, despite promising titles such as *The True Story* and *The Da Vinci Code Unveiled,* most of these works are not particularly reliable. *The Da Vinci Code* itself is not reliable at all. Of course, this may not have been Dan Brown's intention. One should read it as fiction. That is the limited assessment from the serious critics. Or people tend simply to shrug their shoulders.

The relevant question is, Why is *The Da Vinci Code* so immensely popular? The answer is simple: because it deals with Jesus Christ and the claim that the true story of Jesus and his marriage to Mary Magdalene is now finally being told, regardless of what the Church says. In fact it is better not to listen to the Church, according to *The Da Vinci Code.* After all, it has deceived us for around two thousand years.

It is this claim that many people find difficult to accept — the idea that the Church has deliberately deceived us for two thousand years. That is why we read more or less everything that is related to *The Da Vinci Code.* We wish to know the truth. Are these claims true? Is the book fact or fiction?

On the other hand, *The Da Vinci Code* has instigated something truly remarkable. People, especially believers in Christ, have started to ask questions about their belief and their Church. This is a good development, one that belongs to a modern approach to the essential issues of life.

But are there guidelines for examining the basis of religion? Hardly. The Church and theological institutions remain silent on *The Da Vinci Code,* although they ought to accept the responsibility to present their version of the 'truth.' Particularly after the discovery of original texts from esoteric Christian groups from the first century, such as the Nag Hammadi library and the many Manichaean documents. These findings demand a revision of the history of the Church and Christianity. But we are still waiting. This is why the Church, and theology in general, are such an easy target. That is a great pity, because the great question is, Why would the Church want to deceive us for all these years?

In this book, I argue that the Church has not deceived us. It has, however, sheltered us from matters that we were not capable of dealing with, such as evil. According to Saint Augustine, the root of evil is the *motus inordinatus,* chaotic movement. Augustine himself admits that sexual lust led to him being unable to control himself; the flesh rebelled against the spirit.

Sex has always been embedded in religion and rituals. Sex was performed in a religious context, but priests and priestesses had to live celibately. Celibacy is not a Christian invention. Paul would argue that the way to achieve the Kingdom of Heaven was via the spirit not via the flesh. But around the time that Jesus was active, the religious context of sex began to decline. Temple sex became decadent and temple orgies were the result. One only has to recall the Roman emperor, Caligula, to grasp the truth of this statement. The newly-formed Christian Church was stunned by such developments. The Church came to the conclusion that mankind was not capable of dealing with the idea of free sex. It advocated celibacy — sex was only for reproductive purposes. Lust had to be suppressed. This led to problems, of course, as Freud elucidated in the nineteenth century. This ought to have been a signal that it was time for the Church to assume a different attitude. Unfortunately, the Church refused to do so.

The essence of this book is that, with the suppression of sexuality (among other things), the Church has fulfilled a historical assignment. But this mission has now been completed. We are now strong enough to take control of the *motus inordinatus,* regardless of what some television programmes may propagate.

This book does not pretend to be complete. It is more of a brief sketch and could be elaborated on much more profoundly. Nevertheless, it does represent an academic and fact-based approach to esoteric Christianity. In the meantime, I hope that it will function as a worthwhile contribution to the discussion around *The Da Vinci Code.*

John van Schaik
Zeist, The Netherlands
2006

1. The Kiss of Initiation in Antiquity

> Sir Leigh Teabing was still talking. 'I shan't bore
> you with the countless references to Jesus and
> Magdalene's union. That has been explored ad nau-
> seam by modern historians. I would, however, like to
> point out the following.' He motioned another pas-
> sage. 'This is from the Gospel of Mary Magdalene.'
>
> *The Da Vinci Code,* Chapter 58.

The Nag Hammadi Codex

According to many modern followers of esotericism, Jesus was married to Mary Magdalene.[1] The marriage in Cana was that between Jesus and Mary Magdalene. In *The Da Vinci Code,* Dan Brown also claims that Jesus was married to Mary Magdalene. In fact, they even had a child who bore the name Sarah. Brown is actually quite modest, for there are also followers of esoteric Christianity who maintain that Jesus and Mary Magdalene had no fewer than three or four children.[2] As far as I know, the film *Jesus Christ Superstar,* made in the seventies, was the first to suggest that there was a love relationship.

What was the origin of the idea that Jesus and Mary Magdalene had a love relationship? It is taken from two quotes from Gnostic books found in the now renowned Nag Hammadi library. In 1945, a poor farmer discovered a number of docu-ments in a vase in an old ruined monastery. The vase turned out to contain a complete library, hidden in the desert, that once belonged to the Gnostic Christians. In AD 367, the Bishop of Alexandria issued a so-called 'Easter Epistle' in which he listed the books that belonged to the official Christian faith and those that did not. The books that belonged to the official Christian faith were 'good' books, all other books and Gospels

11

were 'wrong,' which included the books that were eventually found in the Nag Hammadi library. Perhaps the believers hoped that better times would come one day.

The notion that Jesus was married is taken from the *Gospel of Mary Magdalene,* which is a part of the so-called *Berlin Codex* (BC) and the *Gospel of Philip* that we know from the Nag Hammadi library. Both gospels contain passages that are used to demonstrate that Mary Magdalene and Jesus had a love relationship. The relevant passages in the *Gospel of Mary Magdalene* are as follows:

> Peter said to Mary: 'Sister, we know that the Saviour loved you more than other women.'[3]

And a little further:

> Peter answered and spoke concerning these same things. He questioned them about the Saviour: Did he really speak privately with a woman and not openly to us? Are we to turn about and all listen to her? Did he prefer her to us? ... Levi answered and said to Peter: 'Peter you have always been hot tempered. Now I see you contending against the woman like the adversaries. But if the Saviour made her worthy, who are you indeed to reject her? Surely the Saviour knows her very well. That is why he loved her more than us.'[4]

Dan Brown quoted this passage in a slightly different variation.[5] Up to this point, there is little than can be disputed. After all, 'loving' and 'making worthy' can mean all kinds of things. Jesus also dearly loved his disciple John. The Gospel of John says: 'One of his disciples, whom Jesus loved, was lying close to the breast of Jesus.' (John 13:23)

However, by linking this passage to the *Gospel of Philip,* 'loving' takes on a different meaning. At least, that is the

view of 'modern esotericism.' We first read the version of Dan
Brown:

> And the companion of the Saviour is Mary
> Magdalene. Christ loved her more than all the
> disciples and used to kiss her often on the mouth.
> The rest of the disciples were offended by it and
> expressed disapproval. They said to him, 'Why do
> you love her more than all of us?'[6]

Now we reproduce the version used by academics, such as
the translation by Luttikhuizen:

> And the companion of the [Lord] is Mary
> Magdalene. [Christ loved] her more than [all]
> the disciples, and used to kiss her often on her
> [mouth]. The rest [of the disciples] ... and said to
> him: 'Why do you love her more than all of us?'
> The Saviour answered and said to them: 'Why do
> I not love you like her?'[7]

Luttikhuizen and other translators such as Slavenberg and
Glaudemans placed the word 'mouth' in square brackets. In
other words, they suspect that this word *could* have been in the
original text, which is a great deal more cautious than Brown's
approach. It also supplies food for thought, because the kiss on
the mouth is crucial to the notion of a love affair. But what if
we consider that we do not really know whether or not Jesus
kissed Mary Magdalene on the mouth? The academic edition
by Robinson is even more cautious. He does not even use the
word 'mouth':

> And the companion of the [...] Mary Magdalene
> [... loved] her more than [all] the disciples [and
> used to] kiss her [often] on her [...].[8]

So we do not know precisely where Jesus kissed Mary Magdalene: the word 'mouth' is simply absent from the Nag Hammadi *Codex*. Jesus could have kissed Mary Magdalene on the forehead or on the cheek. But the suggestion that it was on the mouth does not simply appear out of thin air. It is very possible. We often encounter such an occurrence in narratives from antiquity. It may even have been common practice. Looking at the *Cologne Mani Codex,* for example — a document on the Manichaeans — we read that Mani kissed his father, Pattikios, on the mouth. And tenderly at that.[9] There was plenty of kissing going on in antiquity. For example, Paul wrote that the members of the first Christian communities had to kiss one another with a 'holy kiss' (1Cor.16:20, Rom.16:16). And take Judas' kiss — Judas kisses Jesus, after which Jesus calls out: 'Would you betray the Son of Man with a kiss?' (Luke 22:48).

Jesus may well have kissed Mary Magdalene. Perhaps he did so on her mouth. This does not necessarily mean it was a love affair.

The kiss of initiation in antiquity

Kissing has a different significance. A kiss is an expression of the relationship between the teacher and his pupil. For example, there is the splendid Hermetic document entitled *Discourse on the Eighth and Ninth Heavenly Realms,* which was also found in the Nag Hammadi library. In this treatise, a pupil is taken by his teacher, Hermes Trismegistus, beyond the seven heavenly realms to the eighth and ninth spheres. Hermes Trismegistus is addressed as 'Father' and the pupil as 'Son.' Hermes narrates that he is pregnant from the 'power that swells in him'.[10] This power is spiritual in its nature and bears fruit. Children of the spirit are born. The course of the text indicates that the children are those who have received the Gnosis from Hermes. In the text, they are referred to as the *pneumatici*; the 'spiritual ones.' At the moment that both the pupil and Hermes are drawn into the eighth and ninth realms, Hermes calls out:

> Let us kiss one another in love, O my son. Rejoice
> over this! For already from them the power, which
> is light, is coming to us.[11]

In the adoption into the highest realm, the pupil and teacher become one. The pupil sees the eighth and ninth realm through the consciousness of Hermes Trismegistus. There is a marriage of spirits between the teacher and the pupil, which produces children of the spirit.

A prayer has been included at the end of another Hermetic document, entitled *Asclepius*. The neophytes Tat, Asclepius and Ammon have just been initiated by Hermes Trismegistus into the holy of holies. The prayer precedes the holy meal and ends with the words:

> And when they had uttered this prayer, they
> embraced on another and gave one another a holy
> kiss. Then they sat down at the table and ate a meal
> which was clean because the flesh contained no
> blood.'[12]

The Christian Manichaeans also did their share of kissing. Manichaeism was founded by Mani (216–176 BC). This variant of Christianity developed to become a very comprehensive Church, even reaching out as far as China. Mani taught the idea of dualism. He stated that if God is good, evil cannot come from God. Therefore, in addition to the good principle of God, there must also be a principle of evil. In contrast to the many Gnostic Christian movements, Mani did not teach vertical dualism (above is good, Creation is bad), but rather a horizontal dualism. In other words, good and evil, light and darkness are equally present throughout all the aeons of Creation. This even applies to Creation itself, which contains light and darkness. And light and darkness are also present and interwoven in humans.

Just as Hermeticism and Gnosticism, Manichaeism also teaches that knowledge of the divine, the origins of man, and the future can be obtained by means of Gnosis, by initiation thus. As a consequence, it is not surprising that we encounter the 'holy kiss' in Manichaeism. Many authentic texts of the Manichaeans were found after the Second World War, particularly in Egypt. One of these texts is the so-called *Kephalaia,* in which Mani is educating his disciples. In chapter IX, one of his students asks Mani what the significance is of 'the mystery of the kiss, by means of which one kisses each other.'[13] Mani explains that: The first kiss is the kiss that the *Mother of Life* gave *Primal Man* when he descended into darkness to combat the darkness. It is thus a kind of primal kiss. The second kiss is the kiss the *Mother of Life* and the *Living Spirit* gave *Primal Man* when he returned from the darkness. Both kisses are commemorated among humans. The first kiss when people depart from one another, the second when they meet one another again:

> This kiss exists among people when they kiss one
> another with him (*Primal Man*?), either when they
> go on a journey or when they will to approach one
> another keeping his Mystery (the kiss of *Primal
> Man*) in mind.[14]

It is a rather mysterious text, but later on in the text, in becomes clear what is meant. The kiss is meant for the *electi,* those initiated in Manichaeism who are liberated from the darkness by the kiss. It is an initiation kiss by which fear of the demons vanishes, the heart finds rest, and the *light nous* is born. The *electus* receives the Gnosis from the *light nous.*

Just as in the Gnostic *Gospel of Mary Magdalene* and the *Gospel of Philip,* Mary Magdalene also plays a prominent role in the Manichaean texts. Many Manichaean psalms were found in the Egyptian desert, in addition to the Coptic *Kephalaia*. One of the psalms praises Mary Magdalene as follows:

> Marian, Marian, recognize me: do not touch me.
> (Still) the tears from your eyes and recognize me, I
> who am your Master ... Cast this sorrow from you
> and perform this service: be a messenger for me to
> these lost orphans. Make haste in joy and go to the
> Eleven ... Say to them: 'Get up, let us go, it is your
> brother who is calling you.' If they make fun of my
> brotherhood, say to them: 'It is your Master.'[15]

It is evident that we could regard Mary Magdalene as the first initiate of Christ. She is the first to see him after his resurrection. However, in modern circles, Peter is seen as the one who was not initiated at all.[16] The modern Church is founded on Peter and thus — in a quick deduction — the Church must be exoteric. The *Gospel of Mary Magdalene* is the basis of this assumption, showing that Peter was irritated because the Saviour told Mary Magdalene more than he told the other eleven disciples. So Peter was not initiated. But this is not completely true, because there are also Nag Hammadi texts that refer to Peter as the first Gnostic, as in the *Revelation of Peter*. The Saviour and Peter are sitting in the Temple of Jerusalem, having a discussion. The Saviour says to Peter:

> You too will become perfect, Peter, in accord-
> ance with your name, as I who have chosen you.
> Because I have called you as the first of all to the
> Gnosis.[17]

So, in this text, it is not Mary Magdalene but Peter who is first initiated. The content of the Gnosis that Peter receives is even more interesting. The *Revelation of Peter* is often quoted as the text in which Docetism is discussed in the most pure and visual manner. Docetism is the belief that Christ did not genuinely die on the cross. Just prior to the crucifixion, the Saviour (the living Christ) departed from Jesus's body and stood next to Peter, watching the crucifixion of Jesus. Peter narrates:

> When he had said those things, I saw him seemingly being seized by them. And I said: 'What do I see, O Lord? That it is you yourself whom they take, and that you are grasping me? Or who is this one, glad and laughing on the tree? And is it another one whose feet and hands they are striking?' The Saviour said to me: 'He whom you saw on the tree, glad and laughing, this is the living Jesus. But this one into whose hands and feet they drive the nails is his fleshly part, which is the substitute being put to shame, the one who came into being in his likeness. But look at him and me.' But I, when I had looked, said 'Lord, no one is looking at you.....' And I saw someone about to approach us resembling him, even him who was laughing on the tree. And he was (filled) with a Holy Spirit, and he is the Saviour.[18]

Jesus did not kiss Peter. He could have done so, because there are several Nag Hammadi texts in which Jesus kisses a disciple, as in the *(First) Revelation of James.* James is deep in prayer. Then the Lord appears:

> And the Lord appeared to him. Then he stopped (his) prayer and embraced him. He kissed him, saying: 'Rabbi, I have found you! I have heard of your sufferings, which you endured. And I have been much distressed.'[19]

In the *Revelation of James,* James is given the assignment to spread the Gnosis. James is referred to in the text as 'the brother of Jesus,' but — it is emphasized — not in a literal sense.[20] Here, 'brother' has significance in terms of initiation.

Kissing Church Fathers and martyrs

The above text could give rise to the idea that the kiss only existed among Hemetics, Gnostics and Manichaeans. In other words, it was only used in the esoteric tradition. However, that is not the case. There was a lot of kissing going on among the Christians who represented the later Christian traditions.

First of all, there is Origen (185–254), the Church Father. In the Eastern Christian Church, he is still regarded as the greatest of the Church Fathers, with a stature equal to that of Augustine in the West. Origen came from Alexandria and was familiar with Hermetic and Gnostic initiation practices. This is evident in his commentary on the Song of Songs. This is a mystic commentary in which the human soul is the bride and the Christ is the groom. And because the Song of Songs begins with 'O that you would kiss me with the kisses of your mouth' (S.of S.1:2), the commentary of Origen also begins with kissing on the mouth:

> But let us now quote the words of the Bride herself when her voice is first heard in a prayer: 'O that you would kiss me with the kisses of your mouth.' The meaning of these words is: How long will the Groom send his kisses through Moses, send me his kisses through the prophets? I long to touch his lips, I long for his arrival, for the moment he descends into me. She thus prays to the Father of the Groom and says to him: 'O that you would kiss me with the kisses of your mouth.'[21]

Later in his commentary, Origen poses the question concerning how we ought to understand this. He says: 'Aren't these just stories, if one does not take it spiritually?' It is about 'spiritual love that has its origins in God.' In the same way, the kiss between the soul and Christ is the expression of spiritual love.

This opinion is also held by the Christian martyrs of the same era. In the canonized (official) acts of the martyrs, we find the narrative of the martyr, Saturus. During torture, he has a divine vision. Borne by four angels, he comes to heavenly paradise, where he sees Christ:

> And in the midst of that place we saw as it were
> a hoary man sitting, having snow-white hair, and
> with a youthful countenance; and his feet we saw
> not. And on his right hand and on his left were
> four-and-twenty elders, and behind them a great
> many others were standing. We entered with great
> wonder, and stood before the throne; and the four
> angels raised us up, and we kissed him, and he
> passed his hand over our face.[22]

There is not only mention of kissing in the ascensions of the martyrs or in the mystical unification of Origen, but kissing also takes place in the Christian Eucharist. The (later) ecclesiastical Christians refer to one another as 'brothers and sisters', during the Eucharist.

Justin the Martyr (105–166), one of the first Christian apologists (defenders) and martyrs, wrote about this in his first *Apologia* in the second century. It runs as follows, that: When the community convenes, sections from the Old and the New Testament are read out. Then there is a sermon. The congregation stands up and prayers are uttered, followed by a greeting with a kiss. Then bread and wine are shared.[23]

In the course of the second century, criticism begins to arise concerning the practice of kissing in the Christian communities. Kissing is eventually removed from the congregation rituals, with the result that kissing is later condemned as a heathen practice. Take the Church Father Tertullian, for example (born around AD 155). In his *De Praescriptione Haereticorum* (On the Prescriptions Against the Heretics), he writes:

> I do not wish to omit giving a description of the lifestyle of the heretics. How frivolous, how worldly, how purely human — in the worst sense of the term — this is, without seriousness ... without discipline, just like their faith! To start with, it is not certain who is a listener and who is a believer, they can all gain access on a basis of equality, they listen like equals, they pray like equals ... they share the kiss of peace with everyone who comes .. they are all inflated , they all promise Gnosis. Even the women are rude among the heretics! They have the lack of modesty to teach, to exorcise, perform healings, and probably to baptize as well! Nowhere is it easier to gain promotion than in the camp of the rebels ... because they even allow laymen to perceive the priestly functions![24]

Conclusion

The fact that Jesus kissed Mary Magdalene on the mouth cannot be assumed from the *Gospel According to Philip*. It could be the case, because people in antiquity did kiss one another on the mouth, as an expression of the relationship between the teacher and the pupil, between the initiated and the neophyte. This even applied to men. Mani kissed his father on the mouth. According to the Corpus Hermeticum, it is a 'holy kiss.' The text says: 'Let us kiss in love.' Even in the early Christian communities, people kissed on another before the bread and wine were distributed. But that custom was gradually discredited: it was eventually only heretics that kissed one another.

2. The Mystic Kiss in the Middle Ages and Later

The 'holy kiss' was still important in the Middle Ages, but was different from what it had been previously. It was no longer a kiss between teacher and pupil. The teacher had been replaced by the Resurrected Christ himself. The kiss had become a mystic kiss.

In the twelfth century, Bernard of Clairvaux (1090–1153) developed medieval mysticism. He did this in 96 sermons for his fellow Cistercians at the monastery of Clairvaux. In these sermons, he covered the Song of Solomon from the Old Testament, as Origen had done (*see* Chapter 1). This song, the Song of Songs, the *Super Cantica Canticorum,* is suited *par excellence* to describe the mystical encounter between the Bride and the Bridegroom. The Bride is full of longing for the Groom, she has already laid out her bridal chamber. The bridal chamber is the soul. The Groom can enter there. The discussion between the Bride and the Groom is about their mutual longing for one another. The mystic yearns for Christ and Christ yearns for the one who seeks him. At the same time, the soul is the residence of God as the image of God. Mystics look for God in their soul. They seek what they already possess. Mystics wish to consciously experience the presence of God in their souls. This search is marvellously elaborated with the aid of the dynamics of the Song of Solomon. Medieval mysticism thus means seeking what one already possesses. In the words of the medieval mystic Jan van Ruusbroec (1293–1381): all people have this, only the mystic wants to be aware of it.

The impressively beautiful verse 'O that you would kiss me with the kisses of your mouth' (Song of Solomon 1:2) is treated by Bernard as follows:

Accordingly, I justifiably refute visions and dream images, I do not long for symbols or puzzles. Even the beauty of angel appearances is anathema to me because my Jesus surpasses them by far in terms of form and beauty. Therefore I ask no other, no angel or human, but him alone, to kiss me with the kiss of his mouth. Truly, I do not dare to wish to be kissed by his own mouth: because that is exclusively the joy and exceptional privilege of his adopted humanity. No, much more humbly I request to be kissed with the kiss of his mouth: this is the communal privilege of the many who can say: 'And on his fullness we have received grace upon grace.' (John 1:16)[25]

Beyond the visions and dream images, Bernard seeks the *unio mystica,* that is, kissing in grace. Bernard discusses the dissolving of the soul in the context of no fewer than three kinds of kiss: the kiss on the feet, the kiss on the hand and the kiss on the mouth. The foot kiss sanctifies the beginning of our conversion, the hand kiss is for the more advanced, and the kiss on the mouth is for the few gracious souls. These are, of course, spiritual kisses. Bernard speaks to his monks:

Today we shall read from the book of experiences. Go into your selves and let everyone consider how he is faring with regard to the things we shall discuss, I would like to ask whether it has been given to you to pray in full sincerity: 'O that you would kiss me with the kisses of your mouth.' Not everyone can say that from the bottom of his heart. But those who have received the spiritual kiss from Christ's mouth, even only once, will feel the experience irresistibly drawing and he will yearn passionately for it again. I believe that no one can know that that is except those that

receive it. Because it is hidden manna: only those
who have eaten it hunger for it. It is a sealed well
that no stranger can partake of: only those that
have drunk from it remain thirsty for it.[26]

Hadewych (1210–60) and others

With this kind of introduction to medieval mysticism by means
of the Song of Solomon, it will no longer be surprising that
the 'mystical kiss' of Christ and the mystic is a constant in the
description of mystic experiences.

First of all, there is the Flemish mystic, Hadewych. We know
her from the stories of her visions, her edifying letters to fellow
Beguines, and her strophic poems. In these works, Hadewych
shows herself to be a self-confident woman, a proud soul, as
she herself comments. In her mysticism, Hadewych found
a good balance between reason and emotion. Reason keeps
emotion under control and emotion pushes reason ever further.
This makes Hadewych one of the greatest female mystics. In
line with the teachings of Bernard, Hadewych described the
mystical route in three phases:

1. practise the virtues and meditate on the Holy Scriptures,
   with the result (if one does it properly) that one experiences
   the presence of Christ;
2. enlightenment by means of which one receives visions and
   a first sense of the presence of Christ;
3. unity with Christ in the foundation of the soul.

The various stages merge into one another, not necessarily
in this order of sequence. But the three stages do presuppose
one another. If not, things will go wrong. If one experiences
the presence of Christ in the first phase without practising sufficient virtue, things can easily go awry: *orewoet* (ecstasy) can
be one of the consequences. With this Hadewych means — in
modern terms — that you leave your senses and no longer have

control over yourself, although this is a precondition under all circumstances. You burst out in *jubilation,* clap your hands and forget the rules of the cloister. The result is that you are prohibited from doing the mystic exercises, at least for the time being. You must be fully stable in yourself.

At Whitsun, Hadewych received a vision during matins. She saw an eagle coming from the altar. It told her that she ought to prepare herself for the unification. Subsequently, Christ himself came from the altar, first as a child, then as a man and then 'he came Himself to me.' This all happened 'from outside.' Finally, Hadewych became one with him, and 'he merged and melted in unity with me to the extent that I could no longer distinguish or perceive him outside me or discern that he could not be separated from inside me.'[27] In an increasingly intense series, Hadewych experiences the ultimate unity; the *unio mystica.* At the beginning of the vision, Hadewych imagines what this unification will feel like. It is a 'sweet loving and embracing and kissing.'[28] Christ kisses Hadewych. This is the way she imagines the spiritual marriage. In vision ix, she also refers to the verse on kissing in the Song of Solomon.

The mystical kiss is generally reserved for the last stage of the mystical path. The Spanish mystic, Teresa of Avila (1515–83), describes the mystical path in seven stages rather than three. It is only in the seventh house, as she calls it, that Christ 'draws her to him by means of the kiss for which the Bride yearns.'[29]

There is also the Protestant preacher, Jodocus van Lodenstein (1620–77), who used the metaphor of the Bride and Bridegroom from the Song of Solomon to articulate the mystical relationship between the soul and Christ. In his sermon on the verse in the Song of Solomon concerning 'the king has brought me to his inner chamber' (Song of Solomon 1:4), the 'kiss' is not mentioned explicitly. The only reference to the opening sentence 'O that you would kiss me with the kisses of your mouth' is the following: 'For all this, she (the Bride) praised

Christ and spoke much over his grace, beauty and love.' We are not informed what the king and the bride have exactly done in the private chamber of the king. Jodocus says: 'in this inner chamber he showed her all his magnificence and wealth: he showed Himself and his hidden love immediately, which he had reserved for her long ago.'[30]

The natural-philosophical kiss

In the time that kissing was eliminated from the Protestant mysticism of Jodocus van Lodenstein, it was still going on effusively in another mystical tradition. This is the tradition of the natural philosophical movement. This movement is perhaps better known under the name 'radical pietism', and is also referred to as 'pansophism' or 'Christian theosophy.' This movement includes the alchemists from the seventeenth and eighteenth centuries, as well as the Rosicrucians. Renowned names in this group include Paracelsus (1493– 1541), Valentin Weigel (1533–88), Jakob Böhme (1575– 1624), Christoph Friedrich Oetinger (1702–82), and Goethe (1749–1832). This was an important and vital mystical movement, particularly in Germany. Its characteristic feature was that the participants practised the classical mystical traditions of the Middle Ages — seeking Christ within one's own being. But on the other hand, they also sought Christ in nature. By means of investigation of nature, they attempted to discover the workings of Christ. They assumed that Christ actually exercises an influence on the natural processes, just as he does on the soul. When they look for the 'Philosopher's Stone' in alchemy, or when they try to make gold, these are metaphors for seeking the influence of Christ on nature. In contrast to what our age often thinks about the alchemists, magicians and astrologers/astronomers, they were actually extremely devout Christians. Many of their representatives were preachers or scientists. In the seventeenth and eighteenth centuries, magic and alchemy were 'Arts' — in other words, a science. These natural philosophers were looking for Christ in nature. Present-day science could perhaps learn a thing or two from this approach.

We shall discuss two kisses. First of all, the mystic kiss, as described by Jakob Böhme, and, second, the alchemist's kiss as described by Johann Valentin Andreae (1586–1654) in his *Chymische Hochzeit Christianni Rosencreutz anno 1459.*

The kiss of Jakob Böhme is unique in the history of mysticism. The mystic is not kissed by Christ but by Sophia:

> Dear soul, it must be earnest without renunciation. For the love of a kiss from the noble Sophia in the holy name of Jesus yearns for you, for she is standing in want of it before the door of the soul and knocks.[31]

In the *unio mystica,* the mystic receives a kiss from Sophia, who acts in the name of Jesus. She consummates the marriage and gives the laurel wreath:

> Here the noble woman enters the soul and kisses it intimately with the sweetest love and thus expresses her love in a sign of victory in it (the soul).[32]

Sophia speaks:

> Oh noble Bridegroom, please remain with your face before me and give me you fiery rays. Enter your desire in me and ignite me. In this way, in my mildness, I wish to alter your fiery rays in a white light and bring in my love for your fiery rays in your fiery being, and I wish to kiss you eternally.[33]

Why does Jakob Böhme allow the soul to become one with Sophia and not with Christ Himself? After all, the soul knows that Christ is the ultimate goal, not Sophia. The soul wants the pearl itself, not Sophia's laurel wreath, but Böhme lets Sophia explain the fact that this is impossible. The pearl itself, the *unio mystica* with Christ, can only take place after death, in eternal life. Sophia says that, in this life, she is the image of this union. This means that Böhme is actually more orthodox than the medieval mystics. After all, unification with Christ during life would mean that the mystics believed that one could become divine during one's lifetime. That they could become God Himself. But, of course, this was not possible. Humans remained human. In the fourteenth century, Jan van Ruusbroec was confronted with the fact that he did not always make a sharp distinction between man and God in the *unio mystica*. In his early work, Ruusbroec described the union as a union 'without distinction.' This was heretical because it presumed that man and God had become equals in this union. To avoid that, Böhme placed Sophia between Christ and the soul.

In his *Chymische Hochzeit,* Johann Valentin Andreae describes the union between *Sponsa* and *Sponsus* (Bride and Bridegroom) in alchemical metaphors. The main character, Christian Rozecruce is invited to attend the marriage of the new king and queen. But because we are speaking in alchemical metaphors here, and not in biblical language, it is not surprising that we encounter a different description of the 'kiss.' It is a manner that is convenient for us when we examine the kiss between Jesus and Mary Magdalene in the *Gospel of Philip.*

After the new king and queen have been created as two beautiful statues by means of alchemical labour, they have to be animated. This happens in two stages. First of all, a trumpet is put in both of their mouths. Then a trapdoor in the ceiling of the laboratory is opened and a golden ray of light is poured into the trumpet three times — thus into the mouths of the statues. As a result, they become animated. They are, as it were, wakened by a kiss, just as in a fairytale. This time it is not by a prince but by a golden ray of light as a metaphor for Christ.

29

Then the statues sleep for half an hour. They are not yet awake. Cupid is needed for this: he 'teases them awake behind a curtain'.[34] Have they been kissed awake behind the curtain?

Review: the kiss between Jesus and Mary Magdalene

On the basis of the above text, we can now ascertain that the esoteric, Gnostic and mystic scriptures repeatedly refer to a kiss of initiation, a mystic kiss or alchemical kiss. It is a kiss by means of which the person being initiated becomes one with Christ. What does the *Gospel of Philip* say about this? What does 'he often kissed her' mean? Especially in conjunction with the accusation of the Apostles that 'he loves her more than he loves us.' Does the *Gospel of Philip* say anything about an initiation relationship between the Saviour and Mary Magdalene? To find out more, we must examine the entire text of the *Gospel of Philip*. People often do not do this when they are using this gospel to demonstrate that there is mention of a love affair, although it is absolutely essential! The first important clue in seeking an answer to our question concerning a possible spiritual marriage is to be found in the following text:

> It is not possible for anyone to see anything of those
> that are established, unless he has become like them.
> ... But in the truth it is thus — thou saw something
> of that place, thou came to be among those there.
> Thou saw the Spirit, thou became spiritual; thou saw
> the Christ, thou became Christ-like.[35]

This is a difficult text that describes how the viewer — once in the spiritual world — is no longer engaged in perception and appearances but has become one with them. 'See' still means standing in front of these. Across the threshold of physical perception and the world, you become one with what you see. If you see Christ, you become one with Christ. After all, Christ

30

2. THE MYSTIC KISS IN THE MIDDLE AGES AND LATER

has come to 'rectify the separation.'[36] Man again becomes one when he is born of the spirit, that is when the spirit is reborn through Gnosis and thus becomes one with the soul. [37]

> Therefore the Christ came, so that he might rectify
> to himself the separation that had obtained from
> (the) beginning, by his mating the two together.
> And by his mating them together, he shall give
> their lives to those who have died in the separa-
> tion. Yet the woman mates with her husband in the
> bridal-chamber. Those however who have mated in
> the Bridal-Chamber will no longer be separated.[38]

When the mind and soul have again been united, one has again become a 'perfect person.' These people are referred to as the 'Seed of the Son of Man.' They are the 'Sons of the Bridal Chamber.'[39] They are 'together with the Son of God' and should thus love the Lord.[40]

Like Origen in antiquity and Bernard of Clairvaux in the Middle Ages, the author of the *Gospel of Philip* also uses the Song of Solomon to describe the relationship between the Bride and the Bridegroom. They do so in the mystical mean-ing of the text. The children of the Bridal Chamber must love the Lord. Apparently Mary Magdalene does this more than the other Apostles, and that is why she is initiated by the Saviour. She makes a divine journey to the fourth heavenly realm, as we know from the *Gospel of Mary Magdalene*. Christ is her guide. The text says: 'since it was to this point (the fourth heavenly realm) that the Saviour had spoken with her'.[41] The divine revelation that Mary Magdalene receives is a 'birth.' It is a 'spiritual pregnancy' that the perfect receive:

> For it is by a kiss that the perfect conceive and give
> birth. For this reason we also kiss one another. We
> receive conception from the grace which is in one
> another.[42]

31

Kissing, becoming pregnant and giving birth mean being initiated. Mary Magdalene was spiritually pregnant from the Saviour, and the 'child' is the initiation, the Gnosis, the knowledge of the spiritual world. The kiss allows the spirit, the *pneuma,* to enter. Mary Magdalene is reborn in an enlightened state, just like the new king and queen in the *Chymische Hochzeit* receive the *pneuma* via the light ray from the trapdoor in the ceiling. As a consequence, soul and spirit are united. This is the marriage that is confirmed by Christ.

Conclusion

There was plenty of kissing going on in the Middle Ages. It all took place in the context of the *unio mystica*. The kiss expresses the union between Christ and the mystic. This is also the case with Jakob Böhme, but he saw it differently. In his view, Sophia stands between Christ and the mystic. She is kissed by the mystic. The 'holy kiss' expresses a spiritual marriage, not a physical marriage. 'Spiritual children', not physical ones, are born from this spiritual marriage. This is the way in which the *Gospels of Mary Magdalene* and *Philip* ought to be read: as initiation texts in which the soul weds the spirit.

3. Medieval Grail Literature

'The Grail,' Langdon said, 'is symbolic of the lost goddess. When Christianity came along, the old pagan religions did not die easily. Legends of chivalric quests for the lost Grail were in fact stories of forbidden quests to find the lost sacred feminine. Knights who claimed to be "searching for the chalice" were speaking in code as a way to protect themselves from a Church that had subjugated women, banished the Goddess ...'

Sophie shook her head. 'I'm sorry, when you said that the Holy Grail was a person, I thought you meant it was an actual person.'

The Da Vinci Code, Chapter 56.

Introduction

According to Dan Brown, the secret of the Grail is the secret of the descendants of Jesus and Mary Magdalene. The Grail is the dynasty of Jesus and Mary Magdalene, protected and guided by the illustrious Priory of Sion. Thus, Brown writes about a physical marriage with offspring whereas we, on the basis of the previous chapters, have established that the marriage between these two was a spiritual one. In initiation texts, there is mention of spiritual children. So should we really ask ourselves what the secret of the Grail actually is? Does the Grail conceal a physical bloodline or does it refer to spiritual children? Are we referring to physical or spiritual children?

Much romantic nonsense has been published about the Holy Grail. This chapter will discuss such publications; the significance and the spuriousness of the Grail. It must be emphasized that the narratives on the Grail are only narratives; they form a body of literature. These stories were told at medieval royal courts by bards and troubadours. They were first written down in the twelfth century. The first Grail narrative came from Chrétien de Troyes in 1185: *Le Conte du Graal* (The Story of the Grail). It was as if a river had burst its banks because a genuine flood of Grail stories appeared within a few decades. This lasted until the fifteenth century when Thomas Malory wrote *Le Morte d'Arthur.* How could this literary genre suddenly become so popular? What is the secret behind the Grail?

Chrétien de Troyes

Chrétien de Troyes was born in Troyes in 1135. He was educated to become a priest but became a story-teller and travelled as a troubadour to the courts of the aristocracy relating exciting narratives on the exploits of various knights. Chrétien was mostly in the service of Mary, Duchess of Champagne, and her husband, Duke Henry II. The Duke died in 1181 shortly after returning from a Crusade. Another patron of Chrétien was Philip d'Alsace, Duke of Flanders, so Chrétien was often in Bruges. Chrétien was the first troubadour to write down his stories.

We shall probably never really know how Chrétien developed the Grail genre and where he took it from, but there are some clues. First of all, in the narratives of Chrétien, the knights all have a noble character and are peace-loving. They only fight in cases of severe injustice. For example, there are no fights against the Muslims — which one might expect in the times of the Crusades — or against hostile neighbours. The narratives generally take place in the tournament arena, the place where knights can demonstrate their heroic knightly powers. It was not heroic deeds that appealed to Chrétien but rather the character of the knights. This was a new element in those days and indicated that a different attitude was beginning to prevail; that is, the transition from the early medieval attitude of magical-realism into the attitude of scholasticism and mysticism, in which reason and the individual were gradually developing. We ought to read *Le Conte* in the perspective of transition. King Arthur is described as the ideal picture of the Christian knight. Whereas Arthur's advisor, Merlin, still has one foot in the world of magic of the early Middle Ages — full of wonders and magic — Arthur is a typical Christian reasoner, grounded in scholasticism.

Troyes is only forty kilometres from Clairvaux. Bernard of Clairvaux *(see* Chapter 2) and Chrétien de Troyes are thus active in the same region and in the same spiritual climate. Bernard describes the mystical path in three stages: that of the slave, the mercenary and the son. These three stages resemble the three stages that Perceval undergoes in *Le Conte.* Seeking the Holy Grail is perhaps akin to the mystical path. If this is the case, the programme of the Grail literature is clear. It is intended to convert wild and savage knights into Christian knights, full of noble virtue, loyal to their lady and seeking the Grail. Where Bernard designs a mystic quest for his Cistercian brothers, Chrétien designs a spiritual, Christian quest for the knights. And this becomes popular.

The keeper of the Grail: Joseph of Arimathea

In the same era that Chrétien wrote his *Le Conte,* Robert de Boron wrote another Grail narrative, *Li Romaz de l'Estoire dou Graal.* Robert de Boron was connected to the Abbey of Glastonbury, the place where, according to legend, Avalon was situated. In 1191, the monks suddenly shout *Eureka!* because they have found the grave of the legendary King Arthur. It is pure legend-forming, but it brought the monastery much income due to the many pilgrims who came to Glastonbury (as they do right up to the present day). The monks base their story on the *Historia Regum Britanniae* (History of the Kings of Britain), written by Geoffrey of Monmouth in around 1150. In his book, Geoffrey noted a renowned warlord from the sixth century whose name was Arthur. Whether or not this warlord was ever a king is a topic for the historians. However, it is certain that he managed to unite the British tribes and gain a legendary victory over the invading Saxons in the battle of Mount Badon in 493. Whatever the case, to Geoffrey this was a story about the warlord Arthur who had his place of residence at Tintagel on the coast of Cornwall. Tintagel was once a Celtic sanctuary. An Irish Christian monastery was later built on its foundations, as well as a castle, but it was not a Grail castle. In the writings of Geoffrey there is no mention of the Grail as yet and Arthur was not yet king. It was the monks of Glastonbury who added that part. In this way, fact was changed to fiction.

But there is more. Joseph of Arimathea supposedly landed at Avalon in the time that it was still an island. In *L'Estoire dou Graal* by Robert de Boron, however, it is the son of Joseph, who brings the Grail to Avalon. In *L'Estoire,* we find the story of the origins and the history of the Grail. Robert bases his narrative on Mathew 27:57–60 which tells that after his death Jesus is laid in the grave of Joseph of Arimathea. We read that Joseph was a disciple of Jesus. This produces fine apocryphal stories. The apocryphal *Gospel of Nicodemus* mentions that Joseph was taken prisoner by the Romans and Pharisees and shut up in a tower, where he remained for several long years. People forgot him, but the resurrected Christ did not! In the dungeon, Joseph meets the resurrected Christ in much the same way as Paul did at Damascus. And just like Paul, Joseph did not recognize him at first. Joseph thinks he is seeing a ghost. When he recites the Ten Commandments to ward off the spirit, the ghost recites them with him. Joseph then thinks that he is seeing Elijah. It is only when Christ takes Joseph's spirit with him to his grave that Joseph recognizes him:

> And he wiped my face and kissed me and said unto
> me: 'Fear not, Joseph: open thine eyes and see
> who it is that speaketh with thee.' And I looked up

3. MEDIEVAL GRAIL LITERATURE

and saw Jesus ... And he took me by the hand and
set me in the midst of mine house, the doors being
shut, and laid me upon my bed and said unto me:
'Peace be unto thee.' And he kissed me ...[43]

In passing, we observe that Jesus kissed Joseph, just as he
also kissed Mary Magdalene in the *Gospel of Philip*.

Robert de Boron makes use of the *Gospel of Nicodemus*
but processes the meeting between Joseph and the resurrected
Jesus in an exceptional manner. With Robert de Boron, the
Grail suddenly plays a role:

[Joseph] was not forgotten by God, who is a friend
to man in need. For God rewarded him richly
for what he had suffered. He came to him in the
dungeon and bore the vessel in his hands, which
caused a great illuminated clarity to pour over him
that the entire dungeon glowed with light. And
when Joseph viewed the clarity, he was happy in
the depths of his heart. God brought him the vessel
in which Joseph had caught his blood. In his heart,
Joseph was absolutely filled with the mercy of the
Holy Spirit, when his eye fell on the vessel and he
spoke: 'Lord and Almighty God, whence comes
this great clarity? I believe so fully in you and Your
Names and believe that this light can only come
from you.'

'Joseph, do not be afraid, the power of God
comes to your aid. Know that this [power] will
save you in paradise, where he [the power of the
Holy Spirit] will carry you.'

Joseph then asked of Jesus who he was, because
he was so splendid and light: 'Lord I cannot see
you nor recognize you nor feel you.' 'Joseph,' said
God, 'hear me and believe what I say to you. I am
God's Son, whom God wished to send to the Earth

to save sinners from damnation and from the tor-
tures of hell. I came to Earth to suffer Death, to end
on the cross, to save the work of my Father.'[44]

Robert de Boron further discusses Adam and Eve and original sin, and states that this was the reason why the Lord had to
suffer on the cross. Joseph can hardly believe that he is looking
at Christ:

> 'How can it be, Lord,' said Joseph, 'are you Jesus
> who assumed the flesh of the noble young woman,
> who was the wife and companion of Joseph? Are
> you he for whom Judas received the thirty pieces
> of silver, the one whom they pierced and beat and
> finally hung on the cross? Are you the one whom
> I laid in the grave and of whom the Jews thought
> that I had stolen the body and removed it from the
> grave?'
> 'I am the one, in all truth! Believe me and you
> will receive the Holy Spirit!'[45]

Then Jesus lifts the vessel and hands it to Joseph. Jesus then
gives Joseph the assignment to protect the vessel, which people call the Grail, as Robert de Boron explains a little further
in the story.

It is clear. Joseph sees the resurrected Jesus in the dungeon.
Christ himself confirms that he is the pre-existent Son who has
become incarnate, has died on the cross, and is resurrected in
his glorified body.

Joseph of Arimathea is the founding father of the Grail line.
He sees the resurrected Jesus in the dungeon. This is the secret
of the Grail. The son of Joseph, Bron, is called the Fisher King.
The Fisher Kings are the keepers of the Grail.

The Queste del Saint Graal

The *Queste del Saint Graal* is one of the most well-known Grail narratives, primarily known under its English title *The Quest for the Holy Grail,* which deals with King Arthur and the romance between Guinevere and Lancelot. In the *Quest,* Galahad is the Grail hero who will ultimately become the Grail king. He, too, meets Christ. The *Queste del Saint Graal* was written by the Archdeacon of England, Walter Map (died 1209). He translated the *Quest* from Latin into French on the orders of King Henry II (1154–89). This indicates that the *Quest* originated from before 1189.

Due to fate or the determinations of the spiritual world, Galahad is destined to become the Grail King. In the second chapter, a white monk (thus a Cistercian monk) states that the advent of Galahad can be compared to the advent of Christ.

> Today the similarity is renewed in which the
> Father sent his Son to Earth to free his people. Just
> as foolishness and anger fled at his coming and the
> truth was revealed, the Lord has also chosen you
> among all other knights to travel abroad through
> all countries to end all dangers ... This is why our
> arrival must be compared to the advent of Jesus
> Christ.[46]

Galahad travels through many countries as the new Christ to perform major heroic deeds and liberate people from perilous situations. It takes thirteen, occasionally quite tedious, chapters. The adventure rolls by like a film and Galahad steps in and out, as he pleases, to perform the necessary heroics. However, he remains unmoved by everything he does. It is only in the fifteenth chapter that Galahad arrives at the Grail Castle with Bors and Perceval. In this castle of Corbenic, he meets the keeper of the Grail, Joseph, the 'first Christian

WHY JESUS DIDN'T MARRY MARY MAGDALENE

bishop.' He is the son of Joseph of Arimathea. He gives the host from the Grail as if 'he was serving Mass'.

> When he held the host up, a figure descended from
> above like a child whose face glowed and shone as
> brightly as fire. He descended into the bread which
> clearly assumed a human form in front of the eyes of
> those who had gathered there. When Joseph stood up
> with the host, in full view of everyone, he placed the
> host back in the holy vessel.[47]

Up to this point, this is a well-known medieval theme, which includes a discussion on transubstantiation: is Christ truly present in the host at the *elevatio* or not? To the author of the *Quest,* this is not an issue. He makes it clear that we should place the Grail literature in the context of the Church, not in that of the Cathars, who do not believe in the incarnation, death or resurrection of Christ, and therefore not in transubstantiation *(see* Chapter 4).

However, the narrative proceeds further. It assumes a completely different theme; a mysterious theme because Christ appears once again. Joseph vanishes into the air in a remarkable manner and Christ appears at the same time to the three Grail-seekers:

> When the friends opened their eyes, they saw the
> figure of a man coming out of the holy vessel,
> without clothes and bleeding from his hands and
> feet and side. And he said to them: 'My knights,
> my servants and my faithful sons who have
> reached the spiritual life while they are still flesh,
> you who have sought me so diligently so that I can
> no longer hide myself. It is good that you see part
> of my secrets and my mysteries, because you have
> earned a place at my table at which no knight has
> eaten since the days of Joseph of Arimathea. And

> for the rest, they have received the reward of the
> faithful, which means that the knights of this castle
> and many others are filled with the mercy of the
> Holy Spirit, although never face to face as you are
> now. Take and eat the precious food that you have
> long sought and for which you have endured so
> many trials.[48]

The three companions are subsequently fed by the host that is handed over by Christ Himself. After that, Jesus explains to Galahad that the vessel he is carrying is the one called the 'Holy Grail.' The Grail must be taken by Galahad to the holy city of Sarras, to the 'spiritual palace.' But first Jesus gives Galahad the assignment to heal the ailing King of Corbenic by touching him with the holy lance. Finally, Christ compares the Twelve Knights of the Round Table to the Twelve Apostles. As with the Apostles, he will always be among them. Then Christ rises to Heaven. The next day the three heroes travel with the Grail to Sarras. Galahad is initiated to the status of Grail King. After a year, he asks permission to die and, when he dies, a hand reaches down from Heaven to take the Grail so that no one has seen it since.

The relationship between the Grail and the resurrected Christ is also elaborated in Grail literature in another way. William of Malmesbury is the first English historian to record the deeds of Arthur in his *De Regum Gestis Anglorum* (On the Deeds of the English Kings), dating from around 1125, which was some time prior to Geoffrey of Monmouth. In this work, he states that Arthur's grave has never been found and this is 'why antique fables say that he will return.'[49] This is a direct reference to biblical figures such as Enoch, Melchizedek and Elijah who also ascended to heaven and did not die. This is the reason why the Jews used them as the main characters in the apocalyptic drama of their apocalyptic literature around the time of the advent of Christ. Is Arthur the new Elijah who precedes the advent of the Messiah? And is Galahad, or perhaps

Perceval, the Messiah Himself? In the *Queste del Saint Graal,* a chair at the Round Table is left unoccupied where the Grail hero will one day take his place. It is as if Arthur is waiting for the advent of the Messiah. When Galahad is taken to the court of Arthur, his companion says: 'I bring you the expected warrior who is a descendent of King David.' Arthur is delighted because they have awaited him for a long time.[50]

When the Grail hero has seen the Grail, he becomes the new Grail King. Having become one with the Grail, he is the Messiah. But this time has not yet arrived. Seeing the Grail, Christ, in an uninhibited way is not yet possible in the Middle Ages. The idea of Christ revealing his mysteries is going just too far! That time must still come. That is why God takes the Grail to Heaven. In any case, one thing is absolutely clear in medieval Grail literature: the knights look forward to the second coming of the Son of Man. One day, he will be able to be viewed in an uninhibited way.

Thus the Grail tells the story of the meeting with the resurrected Jesus. That is the true story. Grail knights disperse to seek Christ in the natural world. As medieval mystics sought Christ inside themselves, so the Grail knights seek Christ in the world, through trials and struggles. There is no mystical retreat into their own souls, they go out into the world.

In the *Queste del Saint Graal,* God takes the Grail to Heaven. The question is then: when will the secret of the Grail be revealed? According to Teabing, the evil genius in *The Da Vinci Code,* this ought to happen in the year 2000. At the end of the twentieth century, it should be revealed that Jesus was married to Mary Magdalene and that they established a physical bloodline. This is not the essence of Grail literature, which covers the line of Joseph of Arimathea, and keeps the secret of the direct meeting with the resurrected Christ. It is thus a spiritual secret.

Nevertheless, Dan Brown has touched upon a fascinating theme, although he may be emphasizing the wrong aspect. The fascinating theme is that the resurrected Jesus is again becoming visible in the twentieth century. He is coming closer. Are we sufficiently spiritually prepared to see him? Much literature is currently being written on this topic. Take the book by Hillerdal and Gustafsson, for example, as well as other books with even more descriptions:[51]

> When I had spoken the poem, someone entered the room. I knew immediately who it was. I feel to my knees at the window sill. I did not dare to turn around to view him. He radiated light and peace, which surpassed all reasoning. I clearly felt the touch of his hand, when he bent over and took a burden from me, the burden that I was unworthy to serve as his instrument. I do not know how long I lay there at the window sill.[52]

Could it be that the Grail secret has been revealed in the twentieth century? It is remarkable that people suddenly have a spontaneous encounter with the resurrected Christ in their everyday lives. And perhaps even without undergoing a quest!

Conclusion

Grail knights never really existed in the Middle Ages. There is epic literature for the improvement of savage knights who needed to be Christianized. Instead of engaging in rape and pillage they ought to be spending their time looking for the Grail. During the Quest, knights ought to be celibate. They have to purify themselves. If they are successful, they may find the Grail. What is the Grail? It is a meeting with the resurrected Christ. Whereas the mystics sought Christ in their hearts, the Grail knights seek the Grail in the world at large, but God takes the Grail back into Heaven. The secret of the Grail is the meeting with the resurrected Jesus. This secret seems to be revealed in the twentieth century. If — according to the witnesses — people have a meeting with the resurrected Jesus.

4. Romantic Narratives:
the Grail and the Cathars

In 1933, Otto Rahn published a remarkable book entitled *Kreuzzug gegen den Gral* (Crusade Against the Grail). Rahn was the first to make a link between the Cathars and the Grail. He seeks and finds a historical connection. The main characters from the Grail epic by Wolfram von Eschenbach also turn out to be those in the Cathar drama. He sees Herzeloyde, the mother of Parzival, in Adelaide, the Duchess of Carcasonne. Her son is Ramon-Roger de Trencaval, who is supposedly Parzival himself. In 1241, Parzival surrenders to the Crusaders. The *parfait* (Cathar priest) Esclarmonde de Foix is recognized by Rahn as the Grail Keeper, Repanse de Schoye. And the hermit, Trevrizent, was the alleged model for a Cathar *parfait*. But none of this is true. In *Parzival,* Trevrizent emphasizes that when Parzival arrives at the hermit's settlement on Good Friday it is a reference to Christ's crucifixion. Trevrizent educates Parzival on God who:

> Himself is full of faith. He has always abhorred
> deceit. We ought to show him gratitude because he
> has done much for us due to the fact that his high
> and noble nature has assumed human form for our
> benefit.[53]

God Himself was a child of a virgin, says Trevrizent.[54] Just before Parzival arrives at the hermit's, he encounters a procession of pilgrims. They tell him which day it is, namely Good Friday, the day of Jesus's suffering. They ask Parzival:

> If you believe in his incarnation and in his suffer-
> ing for our benefit on this day, as people respect

> this present day, you are wearing that harness
> mistakenly. Today is Good Friday ... What has
> ever shown more faith than that rewarded by God
> who hung on the cross for our benefit? He gave his
> noble life for our debt.[55]

Could it be more orthodox? The Grail literature is Church literature and belongs to the ecclesiastic Christian discourse. Rahn is a charlatan! Rahn inspired the Thule Community, the so-called 'esoteric' section of the SS. He was expelled from the SS due to problems with alcohol. In 1939, he died under mysterious circumstances on an Austrian mountain.

Rahn was also inspired by Antonin Gadal. Gadal (1877–1962) was the curator of the caves at Sabarthez in the Pyrenees. Accordingly, he could explore the caves as much as he wished, and discovered all kinds of things. The *parfaits* supposedly underwent their initiation rites in the caves of Lombrives. Gadal refers to one of the caves as 'the cathedral of the Cathars.' He called another cave 'Bethlehem.' A large pentagram was allegedly carved out in this one. The parfaits also underwent initiation in this cave, with their arms and legs outstretched so that their hands and feet were touching the points of the pentagram. Gadal describes this in a way as if he himself was present during the medieval rites:

> All the Brothers kneel, except the *Ancien* (elder),
> who has been chosen to take off his pitiable
> clothes. Matthew (the initiation name) now takes
> his place in the pentacle, the five-pointed star, via
> the hollows in the rock. From there he views his
> Brothers who kneel below him: from this moment
> he is their equal. He hears an impressive prayer
> ... It seems as if he has left this world and has
> been taken into heaven ... Oh glorious moment!
> Matthew lives no more: no, he is no longer of this
> world. Suddenly he sees a light, more powerful

than that of the sun, issuing from the hands of the
head of the order. A powerful ray reaches his eyes.
He sees no more than a room bathed in light that
prevents him seeing the bottom ... Matthew can
only call out: 'The cup! The golden Chalice! The
Holy Grail! O Christ, I am prepared. Yes, you only
need to command: just as for you, the sacrifice is
the most previous good ... the golden Chalice ... the
Holy Grail![56]

Gadal is regarded as the secret heir of the last of the *parfaits,* especially in the circles of modern Rosicrucians from the
Lectorium Rosicrucianum.

The Cathar connection is also popular in anthroposophical
circles. The anthroposophist, Déodat Roché (1877–1978), was
an important Grail and Cathar researcher. He was the founder
of the renowned magazine *Cahiers d'Etudes Cathares,* in
which science, religious imagination and esoteric romanticism
are gathered together in a miscellaneous compilation.

The next romanticist is Fernand Niel. He discovered that
Montségur was built as a Cathar sanctuary rather than as a castle. Apparently, a sun-worshipping cult existed here. Exactly on
March 21 a ray of sunshine would shine through a certain win-
dow thus making the Grail visible. But the stone ruin at the top
of the mountain was certainly not built by the Cathars. At the
time of the siege, Montségur was a wooden fortified bastion, a
Castrum. It was demolished after the fall of Montségur in 1244.
A new bastion was built in the same place between 1299 and
1319, this time in stone. It was built by the victors, the persecutors of the Cathars. Anyone who climbs the Montségur full of
respect, with the aim of viewing the Cathar place of pilgrimage,
is visiting a bastion built by the persecutors!

The last Cathars retreated to the caves in Lombrives, in the
foothills of the Pyrenees. There is a large recess in the face
of the mountain through which an increasingly narrow passage, forcing the visitor to crawl, eventually emerges into an

enormous underground cave. This passageway was bricked up in 1328, with 513 Cathars trapped like rats — as the legend goes. Actually the bones found there belong to a group of Neanderthal humans, but it is a fine symbolic end to the Cathars. The Cathar light was eventually extinguished in the caves of Lombrives.

The Gnostic Christianity of the Cathars

Around 1150, the first sources began to mention the Cathars. At the same time Bernard of Clairvaux held his sermons on the Song of Solomon (see Chapter 2), and at around that time, the troubadours were telling their Grail stories in the courts of Europe. The Grail knights were seeking Christ in the world at large, the mystics sought him in their hearts. The Cathars sought Christ in the heavenly realms, just like the Gnostic Christians of antiquity. The Cathar *parfaits* could rise to the seventh heaven. Arnaut Sicre de Ax told the Inquisition:

> There was a *bon homme* [good man, a *parfait*] ...
> who prayed to the Father to show his glory. One
> day, when he prayed in this way, an angel appeared
> to him, saying that he had come to show him the
> glory of the Holy Father ... He took the man on
> his wings and took him to the first heaven which
> comes after this world of misery, and placed him
> there. And this man saw the Lord of this world and
> heaven. He approached him and wanted to worship
> him. But the angel prevented him ... because it was
> not his Father.[57]

The *bon homme* proceeds further. He crosses all heavens until he finally comes to the seventh heaven:

> He [the angel] eventually took him to the seventh
> heaven and when he saw the Lord of that heaven,

> the angel said to him that this was the Holy
> Father and that he could worship him. The man
> approached the Father and worshipped him.[58]

The poor *bon homme* is so overcome with happiness that he does not wish to return to the miserable earth, but he must go back through the seven heavens. It turns out that he has been in heaven for no less than thirty-two years, but measured in heavenly time it is from 'the first to the third hour.' The mystic, Hadewych, also said that she was sorry to have to return from her visions. However, there is a major difference with Hadewych. In the visions, Christ tells her that she has to go back because she has to come to God via incarnation. The Earth is part of the route to God. Our *bon homme* has to return to the Earth for an entirely different reason. The Holy Father says to him that he has to return because 'flesh born from corruption cannot remain there, but must descend to the world of torment.'[59] To the Cathars, the Earth is not the place for meeting Christ, it is rather the place of evil.

The heavenly journey of the *bon homme* is based on a Cathar text with the title *Ascencio Iesaia* (The Ascension of Isaiah). The *Ascencio* is one of the few original Cathar writings, based on the *Ascencio Iesaia* from the first centuries AD. That text probably came to the Cathars via the Bogomils (a kindred Christian sect in the Balkans), and was very popular among the Cathars. The Cathars did cut out one section, in which Christ dies on the cross, receives the glory and, visible to the choirs of angels, travels through the heavenly realms to his Father. In the Cathar text, he also returns in full view of the angels but the Cathars eliminated the reference to 'through death by crucifixion.' The Cathars did not believe in death by crucifixion and the subsequent resurrection. Just like the old Gnostic Christians they could not accept that such an elevated spirit would have contaminated itself by actually becoming one with the 'corrupt flesh.' Not believing in the crucifixion and resurrection is called Docetism (see Chapter 1). After all, the flesh is corrupt and by extrapolation, the whole of creation is corrupt. It is not the good God who created the world but an evil demiurge, frequently identified with Yahweh. He is thus an evil creator and the world is also intrinsically evil. A splendid theological term calls this 'vertical dualism.'

Taking these two items of information in conjunction — Docetism and vertical dualism — means that the Cathars had nothing to do with Grail literature. After all, Parzival learns from Trevrizent exactly what the crucifixion and the resurrection mean. And he learns about the one God who has created everything.

Conclusion

In the Grail literature of the Middle Ages, the narrative is told of the medieval knight who seeks the Holy Grail. When he eventually finds the Grail, it turns out to consist of a meeting with the resurrected Christ who died through crucifixion. The Grail knights see the resurrected Christ during the Eucharist celebrated by the priests. This is extremely un-Cathar. Much of the modern literature on the Cathars assumes that the Cathars were the keepers of the Grail. This cannot be true. The Cathars do not honour the crucifixion, resurrection and the Christian Eucharist.

5. Jesus or Christ in Early Christianity

'At this gathering,' Teabing said, 'many aspects of Christianity were debated and voted upon ... [including] the *divinity* of Jesus.'

'I don't follow. His divinity?'

'My dear,' Teabing declared, 'until *that* moment in history Jesus was viewed by His followers as a mortal prophet ... a great and powerful man, but a *man* nevertheless. A mortal.'

'Not the Son of God?'

'Right,' Teabing said. Jesus' establishment as "the Son of God" was officially proposed and voted on by the Council of Nicaea.'

The Da Vinci Code, Chapter 55.

Man or Son of God?

The issue of whether Jesus was a 'mere' man or the Son of God has troubled thinkers throughout the whole of Christian history. Ecclesiastical Christianity has always maintained that Christ was both; a man and the Son of God. This is referred to as the 'dual-nature theory' as established in the *credo,* the creed. This *credo* acquired its definitive form during the Council of Nicaea in AD 325. But long before the *credo* obtained its definitive form, there were other authorized versions, such as the so-called 'apostolical confession of faith' dating from the second century. This states that Jesus is the Son of God, that he was received from the Holy Spirit and from the Virgin Mary, that he was crucified and died in the time of Pontius Pilate and that he was resurrected. The fact that Jesus was both a man and a God was already evident to the (later) ecclesiastical Christians in the second century, but this does not mean that the conflict had been decided in favour of the ecclesiastical Christians. There were hordes of Christian groups in the second century and they upheld all possible ideas about the 'mystery of Golgotha.' In fact, it has always been the same through the entire history of Christianity. The question about the nature of Jesus Christ arises time and again, and every time it concerns the issue of was he a man or God? The question is still current today, as shown by the Amsterdam professor H.M. Kuitert, who states that the dual-nature theory is a 'failed conceptual model.'[60]

The Council of Nicaea

Dissent about the dual-nature theory in the early Christian Church was the reason for the Council of Nicaea. On the one hand there was Arius (died *c.* 336) from Alexandria, who said that: if Jesus is both man and God it implies that Jesus is also God besides God. Then you have two Gods. That is impossible, according to Arius, so Jesus could never have been God. It was only because Jesus was faithful to God right to the moment of his death that he acquired divine status. Arius's opponent was Bishop Athanasius (died 373), also from Alexandria. He solved the problem by saying that Jesus was one with the Father and thus there is no mention of two Gods. Christ is God with God, not besides God. He was born from the Holy Spirit (divine) and the Virgin Mary (human). This issue led to great controversy in the Church. Arius had many followers, who were referred to as 'Arians.' But Athanasius also had strong arguments which, in his opinion, were more in accordance with the Scriptures.

In the meantime, Emperor Constantine watched this with some dismay. He wanted to ensure unity in his empire and in Christianity. During his reign, from 306 to 338, he favoured the Christians more and more, but it had to be a peace-loving Christianity that propagates unity. To encourage this unity, he summoned all the bishops to gather at the Council of Nicaea. Around 250 bishops participated, of whom only five came from the West. The Bishop of Rome did not attend. To the Emperor, the way in which the Church was organized (in line with Roman law) was more important than the theoretical dispute about the nature of Jesus Christ. Nevertheless, Constantine himself offered the solution by proposing the Greek word *homo-ousios*. This word means that Jesus is 'of the same being' as God. Most bishops could agree to this, but some still saw things differently. They thought that *homoi-ousios* was a better formulation. They added the letter 'i' so that the word meant 'equal in being.' The bishops who could not accept the first solution, *homo-ousios,* were immediately expelled and exiled. Arius was exiled to Illyria. Did this solve the problem? No, the unease remained. So the bishops were summoned again in 327, and yet again in 381 to the Council of Nicaea-Constantinople. However, the bishops could not reach a unanimous theological conclusion and each time a Roman Emperor had to try to maintain order.

What actually happened during these Councils? What did they discuss? Ultimately it was a play on words by the Roman Emperors, a play of legal terms and power, with the intention of controlling matters they did not understand. They were engaged in diplomacy in an area to which it is not applicable. They attempted to understand in rational terms the mystery — which the Church still sees it to be — of the dual-nature theory. This is not possible with mysteries.

The mystery of the dual nature

The Roman Emperors deceived themselves. The dual-nature theory is not a theory, it is a mystery. It cannot be captured in a single word nor rationally understood. If you do wish to do so, you can only choose between the options; Jesus Christ was a man or God. He could not be both. This is because the mind can only think in terms of opposites, in dialectic terms. If something is *this,* it cannot also be *that* at the same time. That is how reason works, but the divine surpasses this restriction. In the extra-sensory world, opposites can coincide. That is more or less the basic concept of the great mystics. Take

Nicholas of Cusa (1401–64), for example, in his *De docta Ignorantia*. The title of the work says it all — 'On educated ignorance.' You only become educated when you have become ignorant; when you can no longer understand things by means of reason. In this way, you are engaged in transcending your reasoning. Then you arrive in symbolic consciousness, in an imaginative consciousness, where opposites can coincide. There, it is no problem that Jesus is both a man and God. But to the understanding, this remains a mystery. The best thing to do is simply believe it.

So, when Kuitert claims that the dual-nature model is a failed concept, he is in fact saying: I argue my belief from the basis of my reasoning. Then I have no choice but to think that it is a failed concept.

However, the Church and theology should amount to more than simple reasoning. To accept Jesus as both a man and as God surpasses reasoning. The power of reason has been enlightened. One must think that the spirit (God) has become (substance) man. One must believe that this is possible! This is true spiritual thought. One step further is the idea that substance (man) again becomes spirit (God) due to the crucifixion. This is true esoteric thinking. The irony of Christian history is that traditional Christianity has always maintained the mystery of the unification of opposites. This is the essence of the confession of faith: 'God became man and lived among us.' In this sentence, traditional Christianity is actually much more esoteric in its nature than the Gnosis or the teachings of the Cathars. After all, the Cathars preach Docetism, as we have seen. They did not believe that God became man and died on the cross.

Who died on the cross?

The Docetism preached by the Gnostics and Cathars contains difficult elements. What does Docetism actually mean? The *Revelation of Peter* in the Nag Hammadi library discusses Docetism in a very visual manner (see also Chapter 1). The

Saviour has just spoken to Peter, after which he is taken prisoner. Peter does not understand what has been said and asks
the Saviour:

> I said, "What do I see, O Lord! Are they really tak-
> ing you away? Are you grasping at me? Who is this
> person I see, glad and laughing on the tree? And is
> it another one whose feet and hands they are strik-
> ing at?"

The Saviour answers:

> The person that you saw on the tree, the one who
> is glad and laughing, that is the living Jesus! The
> other one, into whose hands and feet they are driv-
> ing spikes, that one is the body; he is the flesh-
> manifestation of the immortal being put to shame,
> the likeness perceived by the natural eye. Look at
> him, then look at me."

And thus there is the remarkable scene of the laughing and
joyful Jesus who joins Peter to watch the crucifixion of Jesus:

> Then I [Peter] looked again and saw someone
> approaching that resembled the one who was laugh-
> ing on the tree. He was filled with the Holy Spirit,
> and I knew him then to be the Saviour. And he said
> to me, 'Be strong, you have been trusted with these
> mysteries and their interpretation through divine
> revelation. The one whom they crucified was the
> first-born ... But near the first-born you have seen
> the living Saviour, the first in spirit, whom they
> seized and released, who looks at his assassins with
> joy, while they are yet confused and divided among
> themselves.[61]

It is stated that the Saviour himself, the living Jesus, departed from the fleshly shape that replaces the Saviour. Peter receives insight into this mystery. The Saviour himself provides insight into the truth of the Docetic death. The truth is that it was not Jesus who died but the incarnate form of Jesus. After his baptism in the Jordan, Christ has assumed the veil of flesh of Jesus, as it were, but removed it again just before the crucifixion. The incarnate form of Jesus has died on the cross. Peter is thus not initiated in the Gnosis by the fleshly Jesus, but by the Saviour himself. This is the teaching of the ancient Gnostics and the medieval Cathars. The pre-existent Saviour did not die on the cross, the incarnate Jesus did.

Conclusion

Who or what died on the cross? This is more or less the most important question in early Christianity. How should one view the options? Was it the incarnate pre-existent Son of God? Was it the man Jesus who became divine due to his sacrifice on the cross? Was it somewhere in-between? A bit more God or a bit more man? Was it a god-like man who died, or perhaps a man-like God? Or is there no mention of a combination of the two: does the pre-existent Saviour depart from the man Jesus just before the crucifixion, as the Gnostic teaching claims? Or was there a complete unification on the cross, as later Christianity teaches? Whatever the case, early Christianity maintains that it was the man Jesus who died.

6. Images of Jesus in Modern Theology and Esotericism

Modern esotericism is largely based on ancient Gnosticism in the assumption that it was 'true esoteric Christianity.' Ancient Gnosticism teaches that the pre-existent Saviour departed from the man Jesus just before the crucifixion. The man called Jesus did die, but not Christ (see Chapter 5). It is striking that modern esotericism teaches that the incarnate Jesus did not die on the cross. In ancient Gnosticism, the incarnate Jesus is actually seen as rather unimportant. The emphasis lies on the immortal Saviour or Christ. In modern esotericism — or what is regarded as being so — the situation is reversed. The accent lies on the incarnate Jesus who allegedly did not die.

The incarnate Jesus did not die

The first clear representatives of the 'Jesus-did-not-die' theory were those in AMORC circles. AMORC stands for Ancient Mystic Order of the Rosicrucians, an international Rosicrucian association founded in New York by the parapsychologist H. Spencer Lewis (1883–1939). AMORC issued from the French Rosicrucian-freemason groups; from the French Martinists to be precise.

In 1929 Spencer Lewis wrote an important book, *The Mythical Life of Jesus*, in which he claims that Jesus did not die on the cross. It is an exciting story. Just before Jesus gave up the ghost on the cross, influential followers of Jesus — Nicodemus, Mathaeli and Joseph of Arimathea — came to the cross with a pardon from the Emperor. 'Giving up the ghost' does not mean that Jesus died but that he gave his spirit back to his Father. Just before the Roman soldiers were going to break Jesus' legs (which they have already done to the two criminals next to him), his followers were able to take him down from the cross. Jesus was as good as dead, so they took him to the grave of Joseph of Arimathea. This is where the 'mystic death' of Jesus takes place. But because he is the greatest Avatar of all time, he is capable of recovering quickly from his wounds. As a result, he is the greatest of all initiates, and, in this state, teaches his disciples for forty days. To Lewis, the fact that he subsequently vanishes into the clouds does not mean that he has gone to heaven, but rather that he is going to work in secret. He retreats to a large monastery of the Great White Brotherhood on Mount Carmel. There, his initiates are the Essenes, who become his followers and the apostles. And, of course, the AMORC also belongs to the Great White Brotherhood of Jesus.[62]

What the secret disciples of Jesus actually do is elaborated in Lewis's book *The Secret Doctrines of Jesus,* published in 1937. According to Lewis, those esoteric teachings are still known in the Vatican, but are kept secret. It is fortunate that the old documents containing these teachings are known in the libraries of the Great White Brotherhood in Tibet, India and Egypt. Lewis claims that he takes his information from these, and also maintains that it is time to publicize these secret teachings of Jesus — that is, back in 1937 — in the interests of Christianity. AMORC wished to contribute to the future of Christianity — a noble intention.

Jesus and the Theosophical Society

Jesus as the greatest Avatar of all time is a typical theosophical concept. However, this is not how Helena Petrovna Blavatsky (1831–91), the founder of the Theosophical Society (TS), saw things. She was no great fan of Christianity. Christ appeared relatively little in her substantial oeuvre.[63] To Blavatsky, the entire story of the New Testament is a metaphor for the inner development that every initiate can undergo. The death of Jesus on the cross is, to Blavatsky, the suffering of the higher ego. In her esoteric teachings from 1890–91, she says:

> The reincarnated 'Ray' may, for use, be divided into two aspects, the lower Kâmic Ego is dispersed in the Kâma-loka, the Mâsanic part completes its cycle and returns to the Higher Ego. It is actually this Higher Ego that, to put it this way, is punished, which suffers. This is the true crucifixion of Christos, the deepest and most important mystery of occultism.[64]

Blavatsky leaves unanswered the question of whether or not Jesus was a real historical figure.

This changed with the second generation of leading theosophists, Anne Besant (1847–1933) and Charles W. Leadbeater (1847–1934). Leadbeater was a former priest, so it is not surprising that he paid a great deal of attention to Jesus. He and Besant developed theosophical Christology. Whereas Blavatsky regarded the entire New Testament as a myth of the ancient initiation into the mystery, Besant and Leadbeater declared that Jesus had genuinely existed. In their view, he was the greatest Avatar of all time, and that he will return as the Maitreya Buddha. Leadbeater saw the physical vehicle for the returning Maitreya Buddha playing on a beach in Adyar (India): it was the young Krishnamurti. In secret, Besant and particularly Leadbeater initiated the handsome boy into the secrets of the Great White Brotherhood, which had its centre in the Himalayas at that time. Besant and Leadbeater went even further. That Avatar: that was Christ. Krishnamurti was the vehicle for the reincarnation of the returning Christ. Thus, Krishnamurti was the reincarnated Christ. Many theosophists were astonished and did not want to have anything to do with this Messiah ideology. This was not what Blavatsky had intended! Schisms were the consequence. There were Blavatsky adepts, there were Rudolf Steiner adepts in Germany, and there were many theosophists who joined the Krishnamurti movement. This movement was referred to as the Order of the Eastern Star, and met annually at Camp Ommen in the Netherlands. Some years even witnessed the convention of as many as three thousand followers. But the bubble burst in 1928. Krishnamurti himself rebelled. He declared that he was certainly not the new Christ and that he was not a teacher of the world. In Krishnamurti's view, this is no longer possible in the modern world. Everyone is his own teacher. Besant was broken. The Order of the Eastern Star was dismantled and Krishnamurti began his own movement.

Rudolf Steiner (1861–1925) did the same. From 1902, Steiner had been the chairman of the German Theosophical Society, and was completely opposed to the Krishnamurti affair. Steiner said: Jesus as the greatest Avatar, okay! Of course, the vehicle for Christ must be a very special person. But that is not the same as Christ, the Son of God. He is of a completely different order. Christ can become a man, die and be resurrected in Jesus. Almost all the members of the German Theosophical Society followed Steiner and cancelled their membership in 1913. The foundation of the Anthroposophical Society was the consequence.

The man Jesus in The Da Vinci Code

According to The Da Vinci Code, the notion that Jesus was the Son of God, was one with the being of God, was a fabrication by Emperor Constantine during the Council of Nicaea in 325. That was where Jesus was 'made divine,' says Dan Brown. Prior to Nicaea, people regarded Jesus as a 'mortal prophet.'[65] He was of royal blood, descended from the House of David, and married to Mary Magdalene with whom he had one daughter. Mary Magdalene and their daughter, Sarah, flee when the man, Jesus, is crucified. To Dan Brown, the idea of the divine Christ who dies on the cross is the great deception of the Church. That God became a man is a fabrication. Jesus was at most an exceptional prophetic initiate. That is a part of esoteric Christianity, as taught in earlier times by the Gnostic Christians — according to Brown and many modern followers of esotericism. We now know that the Gnostics had taught something completely different. They regard Jesus as an important 'fleshly vehicle' for the one who is truly important: the Saviour, or Christ, who thus did not die on the cross.

The mythical Jesus in the pagan Christ

The year 2004 witnessed the publication of a book in which the emphasis was placed on this *non-deceased* Saviour. This was the book by Tom Harpur entitled *The Pagan Christ — Recovering the Lost Light*.[66] In this book, the author claims that Jesus never existed and that the entire story of the New Testament should be read as a myth. Everything in the New Testament refers to well-known initiation motifs that were already known in all pre-Christian (pagan) cultures; for example, in the seats of mysteries of Zoroaster in Persia, at the Egyptian initiation sites, in the Greek and Roman holy places. All the themes that were present there in the context of initiation were adopted by the first Christians. Harpur claims that it was all plagiarism![67]

Harpur is not just any old author. He is a professor in the exegesis of the New Testament at Toronto, Canada, as well as being a former priest. He should know, one might say. He is right, of course. The mothers of Buddha and Zarathustra were also virgins, according to the traditions. The God Horus is the Egyptian Christ. The sacrament of the Eucharist was apparently copied from the Roman Mithras mysteries. The early Christians did not invent anything new in terms of rituals. So Harpur concludes that Jesus never existed and that the entire New Testament is the description of a path of initiation that everyone can take:

> The whole Jesus story is the story of each one
> of us, in an allegorical form. Like animals gifted
> with the spirit, we are crucified on the cross of
> materialism, we carry Christ in ourselves and we
> shall one day resurrect for a glorious meeting
> with God. Each soul is crucified if it descends
> into the material body, according to the old eso-
> teric wisdom.[68]

Blavatsky also said much the same thing, but the Church has adapted the story into something else. The Church has deceived us, claims Harpur, for two thousand years. But it has done so in a completely different way from the way Dan Brown sees it. In Brown's view, the deception is that the Church made Jesus divine. Harpur claims the opposite; that the Church has deceived us by turning the myth into a historical occurrence. We see the same distinction in the Theosophical Society. Tom Harpur occupies a position similar to that of Blavatsky, whereas Dan Brown is more in line with the views of Besant and Leadbeater.

Jesus or God?

Is the secret that Jesus has never been God (Brown), or is it the case that Jesus never became man (Harpur)? The problem is as old as Christianity itself, as we have seen.

The ancient Gnostics taught that God or the Saviour never became a man. This is the theory we now know as Docetism. This is also what the medieval Cathars taught, as did Blavatsky at the end of the nineteenth century. By contrast, the Arians maintained that Jesus only became divine after the crucifixion (see Chapter 5), as do the Nestorians. Nestorius was the Bishop of Constantinople in 428, who taught that during his life, Christ increasingly became of 'one will' with Jesus, rather than of one being. His views were condemned by the third Ecumenical Council of Ephesus in 431 because, in its opinion, the ideas of

Nestorius placed too much emphasis on the man Jesus and too little on the divine. Nestorius was exiled to Antioch but that did not prevent the Nestorian Church spreading strongly along the silk route to the east, even as far as China.

However, the idea that Jesus never became God, not even after his crucifixion, is a notion from the mid-nineteenth century. The first theologist who emphasized the man Jesus was the French Professor of Theology, Ernst Renan (1823–92), in his book *La vie de Jésus,* published in 1863. Renan travelled through Palestine and visited all the places where Jesus had allegedly been. This made a deep impression on him; he could empathize with the historical Jesus. In his book, he comes to the conclusion that Jesus had 'earned the divine status that people assigned to him,' but he only received this recognition in the second century, long after his crucifixion.[69] To Renan, Jesus is an exceptional man who was protected and favoured by God. These ideas cost Renan his job. Only much later was it evident that Renan was a very progressive thinker with his notion that Jesus was an exceptional man. Nowadays, this is the generally accepted concept in theology. H.M. Kuitert, professor at the Vrije University of Amsterdam, claims in one of his books that Jesus was a prophet, an extraordinary prophet, because God was active in him.[70]

Around the middle of the nineteenth century, another German Professor of Theology, David Friedrich Strauss (1808–74), propagated a theory completely opposite to that of Renan. In his book, *Das Leben Jesu* (The Life of Jesus), published in 1835, he claimed that the New Testament did not deal with the historical Jesus but rather with what people made of this. Perhaps the book ought to have been called 'The Mythical Jesus.' In his view, the first Christians pasted their ideas of the mythical (divine) Christ onto the historical person of Jesus. Poor Jesus! In his day, Strauss resisted the hype of the historical Jesus research. This hype has never ceased since then. To Strauss, a historical Jesus is completely unnecessary in order to believe in the mythical Christ. In doing so, Strauss is the first to split the Son of God from the historical figure of Jesus. But he does so from the other direction than Renan would do a few decades later (from the human side). These viewpoints have never been reconciled.

Spirit (the Son of God) or substance (the man Jesus)

From the middle of the nineteenth century, we see that the dual-nature theory is attacked from two sides. Strauss undermines the 'one being' idea from the mythical side — you can still believe in the mythical Christ without believing in the historical Jesus. Renan attacks the 'one being' theory from the human side. In his view, it is all about the exceptional figure of Jesus. Renan makes Jesus Christ, the Son of God, a physical person. Strauss restricts himself to a purely spiritual interpretation. The idea that the Son of God could become a man — the spirit could become substance and *vice versa*, could again become spirit (after the crucifixion) — is no longer tenable after the middle of the nineteenth century.

In this way, we can see two paths in present-day esoteric Christianity, two types of concepts. The so-called esotericism of Dan Brown in *The Da Vinci Code* displays a purely historical approach, while Tom Harpur restricts himself to dealing with the myth. The fact that this myth has been taken to be a physical Jesus is, in his opinion, the deceit of the Church.

Jesus and Christ in anthroposophy

Only ecclesiastic Christianity has always maintained that there is mention of two states, God and man, spirit and substance. This is true esotericism, but can only be understood if one goes further than reasoning allows. The Church has not done so (see Chapter 5). As a consequence, the Church no longer understands its own esotericism; it must simply be believed. In itself, belief is a splendid thing but it is no longer enough.

So the dual-nature theory is attacked from all sides without the Church offering sufficient resistance to these assaults.

There is one modern esoteric movement in which the emphasis is placed exactly upon the dual-nature theory, the crucifixion and resurrection. According to Rudolf Steiner, the founder of anthroposophy, the dual-nature theory can only be understood when one develops reasoning to a higher level of comprehension. Without conceding one's critical capabilities as such, Steiner developed a mystical path that leads to insight in the spiritual world, where one can perceive the unity of opposites. There, it is not strange that spirit and substance are one, and that Jesus and the Son of God are one. Steiner says:

> It was the lot of the Christ Being to feel how the Divine power steadily waned in this process of self-assimilation to the body of Jesus of Nazareth. Stage by stage the God became a Man. Like someone who in the throes of unceasing pain becomes aware that the body is steadily declining, so was the Christ Being aware of the waning of His spiritual power while as an etheric Being He was gradually identifying Himself with the earthly body of Jesus of Nazareth ... until the similarity was so complete that He could feel anguish like a man. ... In the same measure in which this etheric Christ Being grew to greater identity with the body of Jesus of Nazareth, in the same measure did the Christ become Man.[71]

According to Steiner, the incarnation, crucifixion and resurrection are the central occurrences in the entire development of the world and humanity. Steiner also says:

> The actual sacrifice of the Christ being lay in the departure from the spiritual realms, in order to live on Earth and with the people on Earth, and to

advance humanity and the evolution of the Earth
by giving it this impulse.[72]

That is why it could only happen once. The return of the
resurrected Christ does not take place in a physical form but
rather in what he calls an 'ethereal' body. This is the glorified resurrected body. Steiner predicted that at the beginning
of the twentieth century that the time of the Second Coming
would begin. He maintained that anthroposophy was meant
to prepare the return. With this form of Christology, Steiner
seems to be closer to the old *credo* than present-day theology.
This is also why, in 1913, Steiner broke definitively with the
Theosophical Society, which held a completely different view.
Anthroposophy is thus not a form of theosophy but rather a
kind of esoteric Christianity.

Conclusion

The problem of the dual-nature theory has spanned the entire
history of Christianity. People tend to lean to one side or the
other: He was a man and was made divine by the crucifixion;
or No, he was (the Son of) God and became a man. Only
ecclesiastical Christianity has always maintained that both are
possible: God and man. This is true esotericism, but can only
be comprehended if one goes further than one's reasoning
allows. The Church has not done so, and, as a consequence, the
Church has not understood its own esotericism; the teachings
had to be simply believed. This has meant that the dual-nature
theory has been attacked from all sides without the Church
being able to offer any resistance. Strangely enough, those
who follow the anthroposophy of Rudolf Steiner uphold the
idea of the dual-nature theory, which can be understood if one
develops reasoning to a higher level.

7. To Gnosis via Sex?

'Specifically, the Church accused the Templars of
secretly performing rituals in which they prayed to a
carved stone head ... the pagan god ... [Baphomet].' ...
　　Langdon quickly explained to Sophie that Baphomet
was a pagan fertility god associated with the creative
force of reproduction ...
　　'The ceremony honoured the creative magic of
sexual union.'

The Da Vinci Code, Chapter 76

Sexual rites among the Canaanites, Christians, Gnostics and Manichaeans

The Old Testament contains a story over the Canaanites who
apparently performed sexual rites; at least that was how the
Jews saw it. The Book of Wisdom states:

> Those who dwelt of old in thy holy land
> thou didst hate for their detestable practices,
> their works of sorcery and unholy rites,
> their merciless slaughter of children,
> and their sacrificial feasting on human flesh
> 　and blood.
> These initiates from the midst of a heathen cult,
> these parents who murder helpless lives,
> thou didst will to destroy by the hands of our
> 　fathers (12:3–6).[73]

According to the Romans, the Christians also performed
sexual rites:

67

They recruit from the dregs of the population
nitwits and credulous women who solely by their
gender are unstable and easily influenced. They in-
volve the multitude in a godless conspiracy which,
by means of nocturnal meetings, regular periods
of fasting and food not fit for humans, unites the
people in genuine wrongdoing, a people that is
active at night and avoids daylight, which is silent
in public but has much to say in dark alleyways
... This conspiracy ought to be exterminated at
the roots and cursed. They recognize one another
by secret signals and signs and make love to one
another before even knowing one another. Together
they participate in a kind of Cult of Lust without
any regard for one another's status and call one another 'brothers' and 'sisters' ... Some people claim
that they worship the genitals of their priests and
high priests, and that they worship them like those
of their fathers ... A child is covered with flour to
mislead the unsuspecting ... The child is killed in
its innocence by the neophyte ... The blood of the
child ... they lick up greedily. They fight one another for the limbs of the child ... These rituals are
more disgusting than all sacrilege.[74]

So this is what the Romans thought of the early Christians.
This is understandable. After all, in the vision of the Romans,
don't they worship a dead person and drink his blood and eat
his body? Cannibalism of the purest kind!

But according to the later ecclesiastical Christians, it was
the heretical Gnostic Christians who performed the sexual
rites. In his *Panarion* (medicine cabinet), Bishop Epiphanius
of Salamis (315–403) wrote that the members of the Gnostic
sects recognized one another by means of secret signs. In addition, they ate human flesh during their liturgy and had sex with
one another:

> Although they have sex with one another, they
> forbid the generation of children. So they yearn
> for the depraved deed not to generate children but
> rather for the pleasure ... And when they are fin-
> ished, they eat the seed of their uncleanliness ... but
> if the woman becomes pregnant ... they abort the
> foetus and crush it in a mortar with a pestle, then
> mix the foetus with honey and pepper and other
> herbs and sweet oils ... Then all the members of
> this perverted sect lick this mixture.[75]

It is a bit of a monotonous story, but according to Augustine (354–430) it was the Christian Manichaeans who indulged in sexual rites. In his *De Haeresibus* ('On the Heretics') the story is much the same: they use sperm as a kind of holy feast, and more of that type of excesses.[76]

Heretics and Cathars in the Middle Ages

People continued with this kind of activity in the Middle Ages, but then, of course, it was only the Church that fulminated against all type of heretics who were engaged in wild activi- ties. For example, the monk Adémar of Chabannes (998–1034) wrote about the heretics in Orléans in 1022. He referred to them as Manichaeans, but they did not belong to this group. They were pious Church reformers who were more strict than many of their Church brethren and pointed out many injustices in the Church. They accused the Church of no longer living according to the teachings of Jesus. Bishops and abbots were fat, rich and not celibate, so protest was the result. This was regarded as a threat to the Church authorities, so these pious laymen were quickly marked as Manichaeans, arch-heretics *par excellence*. This is what Adémar of Chabannes read in *De Haeresibus* by Augustine, whose works were in the library of the Saint-Cybard monastery in Angoulême. According to Adémar, the heretics in Orléans were called 'Manichaeans' by:

'a farmer from Périgord who claims he can perform miracles and who carries the ashes of dead children with him.' The heretics 'worship the devil ... and practise abominations and crimes of which it is too grave even to speak.'[77]

The monk restrained himself, but that was not the case with the abbot of the monastery in Nogent, Guibert de Nogent (1053–1124). He wrote about heretics — whom he also referred to as 'Manichaeans' in Soissons in around 1114. We read:

> They hold meetings in basements and secret
> places, men and women together. When the
> candles have been lit, women of easy virtue, with
> bare buttocks, offer themselves — in full view of
> everyone — to a certain person who is positioned
> behind them. The candles are directly extin-
> guished and everyone shouts 'Chaos' and every-
> one has sex with everyone who is available. If it
> happens that a woman bears a child, that child is
> brought to this same place as soon as it is born. A
> great fire is lit and the child is thrown from hand
> to hand across the fire by everyone sitting around
> the fire until it is dead. From its ashes they then
> make bread of which a gruel is given to every-
> one as a sacrament. When this has been eaten, it
> seldom happens that people regain their reasoning
> from this heresy.[78]

In around 1182, Walter Map — the author of the Grail narrative on Arthur, Galahad, Lancelot and Guinevere — wrote
about the Publicans, or Patarines, in Aquitaine and Burgundy.
These are the Cathars. The members of 'this old heresy' meet
at night in their synagogues. This does not refer by definition to Jews. The word 'synagogue' was occasionally used to
describe the meetings of heretics. When all the doors, win-
dows and other openings have been sealed, the group inside

awaits the arrival of a black cat of enormous dimensions. When they have found the cat in the dark they kiss and worship it. Then everyone grabs the adjoining man or woman and they have sex with one another until everyone is completely satisfied.[79]

Long before the Templars were accused of such practices, there was a whole *corps* of fantasies about 'the others.' We find exactly the same accusations in the reports of the Inquisition on the confessions of the Templars.

The Templars

The Templars, too, were accused of performing sexual rites. At least, that is what they confessed during the Inquisition. But, of course, this was under the coercion of torture that was by no means half-hearted. Perhaps this was the first time that the group that was accused of depraved sexual practices actually admitted it. Of course, it was all written down by the Inquisition.

Just as with the Cathars and the Grail, modern literature on the Templars is clad in a veil of esoteric romanticism. They too were thought to belong to the Grail Keepers. The Order of the Templars was founded in 1119 with the aim of protecting the pilgrims on their travels to the Holy Land. In medieval sources, a certain Hugues de Payens is named as the founder of the Templars. Hugo is a noble lord from the Champagne region, only thirty kilometres from the city of Troyes. Troyes was also the birthplace of Chrétien de Troyes who wrote the first Grail narrative. The family of Hugues de Payens was also on friendly terms with Bernard of Clairvaux. The mysticism, the Grail literature and the idea of Temple Knights could well have come from one communal domain. The Cistercian monk Bernard was also a proponent of a holy war against the Muslims, and was a great champion of the Second Crusade. So it is not surprising that Bernard actively supported the objectives of the Temple Knights at the

Council of Troyes in 1128. During this Council, the Order of the Knights Templar was officially founded and received official status. Bernard played an important role in this. He wrote about it in his treatise entitled *De laude novae militae* ('In praise of the new military').[80] In this book, Bernard developed the concept of the knight-monks. He concluded the treatise with the words:

> I do not know whether I should call them 'knights'
> or 'monks.' And how could you identify them
> better than by means of these two names together,
> those men who lack neither the mildness of the
> monks nor the bravura of the knights.

So the Templars are both knights and monks. They adhere to the same rules as the monks. The new Order fights on two fronts, according to Bernard. This fight on two fronts is succinctly articulated by Abbot Guigo of the Carthusians. In 1128, he sent a letter to Hugues de Payens:

> After all, it is useless to attack external enemies if
> one has not first harnessed one's inner foes ... Let
> us first produce our own fight. Only then can we,
> in all stability, take on our enemies in the outside
> world. First we must purify our souls of their
> iniquities and then we can purify the Earth of the
> barbarians.[81]

Like the Grail knights in the Grail literature of a few decades later, the *militia christi* (the knights of Christ) were also expected to be celibate. It is remarkable that, during their torture in 1307, they were accused of exactly the opposite by the Inquisition. It is even more striking that *The Da Vinci Code* maintains that the Templars indulged in sexual rites. For this Dan Brown based his text on the interrogations by the Inquisition, which all of a sudden are apparently valid sources, although Brown forcefully rejects the Inquisition elsewhere. But that is a digression.

What exactly happened during the persecution of the Templars in 1308, almost two centuries after the order was founded? As early as 1305 there were stories of heresy, idolatry, and sodomy among the Templars. The Pope didn't believe them. He even planned to set up a study with the aim of exonerating the Templars, But then Philip IV ('Philip the Fair'), King of France, interceded. On October 13, 1307 he gave the order to arrest all the Templars in France and confiscate their goods. The Pope was dismayed at this occurrence and undertook to seize the initiative by ordering their arrest himself. He must have thought that the Templars would be better off at the ecclesiastical courts than at Philip's secular courts, but the consequence of his action was that the Templars were arrested throughout the entire Christian world. It is remarkable that the Templars offered little or no resistance. There was no way back, for shortly after their arrest, Philip produced the renowned incontestable confessions of the tortured Templars.

The confessions of the Templars amount to the following: they renounce Christ and spit and urinate on his cross; they worship idols, especially a cat called Baphomet that they supposedly kiss on the anus; they do not believe in the sacrament of the Church; they give absolution although they have not been initiated; they perform sexual rites and indulge in homosexuality. Under torture, even the Grandmaster of the Order, Jacques de Molay confessed. The Inquisition report of October 24, 1307 is as follows:

> He also said under oath ... that the person who took him in (on his becoming a member) brought him a bronze crucifix with the image of Christ and told him to renounce Christ whose image was before him ... When asked if he remembered, when he took his oath of celibacy, that people had told him to unite with his brothers in the flesh, he answered

under oath that he could not remember this and had
never done this .... However, he did declare under
oath that when he had taken in brothers he had said
to a few of his assistants to take the new members
apart and to allow them to do what they had to
do.[82]

The Inquisition reports are full of accusations of homosexuality; the brothers do it with one another. There is hardly
any mention of women anywhere. There is no reference to
hiëros gamos, holy union between the Templars and women.
At least, there is nothing on this in the Inquisition reports that
Dan Brown uses. And it is not the Pope but rather the King of
France that destroys the Order.

Most Templars withdrew their confessions after a time. But
that did not help, the damage was done; the confessions were
there and could be undone. And anyone who was not against
the Templars — like the Pope — was for them, at least in the
eyes of Philip, and was therefore a suspect himself.

Ordo Templi Oriento

Dan Brown has an error margin of around seven centuries. It
was not the Templars that indulged in sexual rites but the Ordo
Templi Orientis (OTO). This was not in 1300 but rather in
1900, in Germany and later in England. The OTO was founded
by Theodor Reuss (1855–1923), William Wetscott (1848–
1925) and John Yarker (1833–1913). In the OTO, they wished
to design and practise extremely occult (secret), irregular,
free-mason rites. It is a complicated story. Initially, the OTO
functioned as a system of secret degrees within the Memphis
and Misraïm order of free masons, of which Rudolf Steiner
was the Grandmaster in Germany from 1906–14. But in 1907,
Steiner emphatically distanced himself from Yarker and Reuss.
He writes on this in his autobiography *Mein Lebensgang* (The
Course of my Life). This was a good development because at

that time, rumours were beginning to circulate that Reuss was engaged in sexual magic, and was the reason that he fled to England. In London, Reuss met Aleister Crowley (1875–1947) who was also referred to as the Grandmaster of Sexual Magic. Reuss and Crowley founded an independent OTO in London. The OTO was known as the society in which sexual magic was openly performed. Crowley even called himself 'Baphomet.' Baphomet wrote books about those sexual practices. In his *Exercise Book for Astral and Symbol Magic* he wrote:

> According to esoteric teachings, God opened himself with a certain generative joy, thus procreating in a sensual way, so the harmonious indulgence in sexuality is an original act and of pure divine origin.[83]
>
> The medium must be lying in a comfortable state of rest, with her head toward the south, thus opposite to the magnetic Earth meridian. You will understand that the position of the medium is extremely suitable and makes her more receptive. The medium must be naked, and be in a completely healthy and harmonious state. In addition, you must ensure a high room temperature. You protect yourself by means of a pentagram on your forehead and a black silk cloak. On your breast, you wear your cosmic glyph, which you must have calculated yourself in accordance with the magic numerical squares. When you have performed the incense ceremony, with hash or a similar narcotic powder, you bring the medium into the well-known charm state and close the place of rest of the medium off by means of a special new magic circle. Then, sitting cross-legged, to sit down next to the medium and you bring yourself into a trance by means of yoga breathing exercises which liberate mental vibrations ... when this has happened, you

> waken the medium from the charmed sleep; lift her
> up and pull her onto your lap to perform the act
> of union. Take care that, after the deed, the sperm
> leaves the vagina and mixes with the spirit of the
> wine, so that the mystic union is also fulfilled
> inside the formed being.[84]

The result of this magical sex is ultimately that a magical astral being is created. Crowley calls this being a 'phantom' that has to be destroyed again after some time.

It is now clear to me where Dan Brown obtained his idea of sexual magical practices. Not from the Templars but from Crowley! And the OTO has nothing to do with the medieval Templars, even though their name may give that impression.

Conclusion

The stories of weird sexual rites in antiquity are mainly narrated by others. The Jews accused the Canaanites, the Romans, the Christians, the (ecclesiastical) Christians the Gnostics and the Manichaeans. In the Middle Ages, people happily pursued this line; all heretics indulged in these rites, and so did the Templars. After all, they confessed it under torture of the Inquisition, even though they soon retracted their statements when they had the opportunity. It was only in 1900 that there was an association that openly wrote about magical sexual rites — the OTO, founded by Aleister Crowley. Did Dan Brown base his passages on this order?

8. Temple Virgins and the *motus inordinatus*

In the old pre-Christian schools of mystery, sex was embedded in a religious and astrological/astronomical context. Only with certain configurations of the stars were offspring generated. These were not 'ordinary' offspring, but rather 'holy children.' The so-called *hiëros gamos* that Dan Brown talks about probably has this objective, rather than the sexual mystical union with the divine. The Church Father, Augustine, speaks full of admiration of the Roman Vestal Virgins:

> A Vestal Virgin, who was embroiled in a dangerous process because she was unjustly accused of indecency, apparently filled a sieve with water from the Tiber and brought it to her judges without any of the water leaking away. What was it that held the weight of water in the sieve? They would have answered: some or other god or demon.[85]

and:

> Priestesses of Vesta caught performing indecent acts were buried alive by the Romans themselves, while adulterous women were given punishment but never had to pay for their crimes with their lives. They defended what they regarded as the sacredness of the gods with so much more emphasis than the marriage bed of the people.[86]

As virgins, the Vestal Virgins could make predictions. Then the divine power evidently spoke through them and the works of God stopped when the maidens were no longer virgins.

This was why the Romans took such care to keep the maidens virgins. The temple priests were also celibate. We know this from the Isis mysteries of late antiquity. In the narrative *The Golden Ass,* Apuleius describes (in the second half of the second century) how a certain Lucius was initiated into the mysteries. In the preparations for the ultimate initiation rite, he has 'meticulously investigated how strict the refusal of all sensual pleasure' is.[87]

But the Jews also had virgin temple priestess. The Virgin Mary was apparently one of them, at least, this is the case according to the apocryphal script entitled *The Birth Of Mary,* also known as the *Proto-Gospel of James.* These writings were already known in the middle of the second century and were very popular in the Middle Ages. The text deals with the birth of Mary, her youth, her marriage to Joseph and the birth of Jesus. When Mary was three years old, her parents Joachim and Anna gave her to the Temple. On arriving at the Temple Joachim calls out:

> Let us call the pure women of the Hebrews. Let
> them take up lamps and light them so that the child
> will not turn back and her heart will never be led
> away from the temple of the Lord.[88]

So there were 'pure women.' The three-year-old Mary danced on the stairs to the Temple, by which she stole the hearts of the whole House of Israel. In the Temple, Mary was fed by an angel. When she was twelve years old, the priests looked for a widower for her. They found Joseph. A dove emerged from his staff. This was an omen that God had chosen him to 'look after the Virgin.' But he was explicitly forbidden to have sex with her. The words 'look after her' are used consistently. Mary moved in with Joseph (and his sons). After a while, Joseph went away to build a house. While he was away, Mary worked as 'one of the virgins of the tribe of David' on a new curtain for the temple. Joseph

was away for six months and in that time Mary became
pregnant by God:

> Shall I become pregnant from the Lord, the living
> God, and shall I bear a child like all other women
> bear children.

She is sixteen and hides at the house of Elizabeth in shame.
When Joseph returns, he is deeply unsettled. Who has made
her pregnant? He calls out:

> How can I look to the Lord God? What will I pray
> about her, for I took her as a virgin from the temple
> of the Lord and did not guard her? Who has set this
> trap for me? Who did this evil in my house? Who
> stole the virgin from me and defiled her?

It is clearly not Joseph who has made Mary pregnant. Joseph
is distraught but fortunately an angel comes to inform him that
Mary has been made pregnant by the Holy Spirit. The priests
are agitated and accuse Joseph of making the virgin pregnant.
Joseph and Mary are called to justify themselves to the priests.
A priest speaks:

> Mary, what is this? How have you humiliated your-
> self? Did you forget the Lord your God, you who
> were raised in the holy of holies and received from
> the hand of an angel? You who heard their songs
> and danced before them, what is this?

Mary apparently ought to have remained a virgin, even if
she is under the protection of Joseph. She is still in the service
of the temple, where she danced.

Joseph and Mary proclaim this innocence. They are put on
trial by the priests. They are made to drink 'test water' and are
sent into the desert, but they return unharmed. The conclusion

79

is that they have not sinned and they may return home. A short time later, Jesus is born.

What can we conclude from this story? Whatever the case, we can say that Joseph did not make Mary pregnant, that was the responsibility of the Holy Spirit. A virgin temple priestess becomes pregnant by the Holy Spirit. She has been brought up in the most holy of surroundings, where God lives. God made her pregnant. The 'power of the Lord will overshadow her,' it is written. Her son is the 'Son of the Almighty.' Of course she must have been made pregnant in a natural way. If that were not the case, Jesus would not have possessed human nature. Exactly who has made her pregnant is not clear in the text. But the fact that this has taken place in a temple context is quite clear. 'Virgin' means that it refers to a spiritual context, not to a physical context. There is no mention of lust. In this way, Jesus is a Son of God. This is what the holy men that were generated in this way were called in antiquity. In other words, there were many sons of God in those days. People knew that they came from the temple.

The angst for disorder

In the same time as the apocryphal gospel on the nativity of Mary, the spirit of lust began to make itself felt. Priest-supervised procreation in the temple, with the aim of producing Sons of God, became profane. Roman Emperors also began to refer to themselves as 'sons of God.' Or even God. There is an inscription from Asia Minor dating from 9 BC in which Emperor Augustus (ruled from 27 BC to AD 14) was praised as 'Saviour' and God. The sexual temple practices become decadent. We only have to look at the Emperors Caligula (ruled from AD 37–41) and Nero (ruled from AD 54–68). Without any preparation, they allow themselves to be initiated in the various temple mysteries and are notorious for their exuberant sexual orgies. This requires little argument. It is exactly this sexual decadence that the Christian Church attempts to challenge by trying to keep sex in a priestly context. As Paul said: not in matters of the flesh but in matters of the spirit, that is where one finds God. By living in accordance with the spirit. This is why holy men have to live a celibate life. This is quite common in antiquity.

Why is this so? This is because people are afraid of the *motus inordinatus,* the chaotic movement of the flesh. This is a concept propagated by the Church Father Augustine, but he took it from the Manichaeans (see Chapter 1), who taught that there were two principles at the beginning of everything; God and *hyle,* or God and Chaos. *Hyle* is characterized by the *motus inordinatus.* This is ultimately the source of chaotic sexual lust. The Manichaeans placed the origins of this chaotic sexual lust right at the beginning, in the divine realms, as the counterpart to God.[89] Augustine protests against this idea as he designs the idea of original sin. He says that: Evil cannot be found in the primal cosmic beginnings, but rather in man. It began with Adam and Eve. They knew one another as a result of the movement of chaos, whispered to them by the Devil. 'That was when the flesh began to feel lust, against the principles of the spirit,' says Augustine.[90] When Adam and Eve sinned, 'they experienced a previously unknown movement of their disobedient flesh,' because the soul — which was disobedient — was separated from the body, so that the flesh took on its own movement: a chaotic movement, the *motus inordinatus.* This is the source of the Christian denial of 'the flesh,' the body. The body is our enemy.

So, at the beginning of the Christian era, two things happen with regard to sex:

1. sex begins to free itself from the priestly context, at least, this is the case where it concerns the initiates and the priests and priestesses;
2. with the teachings of Augustine, the roots of sexual lust are ascribed to man himself instead of them being present in the primal beginnings, as postulated by the Manichaeans.

Man himself is the cause of sexual lust and sex is released from its religious-ritual context. The Church subsequently concluded that: man cannot yet accept this state of affairs! So, they advocated celibacy for the priests. The spiritual leaders of the people ought to live in harmony with the spirit, which means that they ought to be celibate. To church-goers, this meant that sex was only for procreation. The *motus inordinatus,* sexual lust, must not play a role under any circumstance. The Church has always warned us that this is sinful. The Church has always been afraid that sexual lust would overwhelm people, that we would surrender to all kinds of temptation. And rightly so. Look at some commercial television stations. Is it not the case that the historical duty of the Church is to protect us, by offering some kind of moral counterweight? Hasn't the Church given us the opportunity to mature inwardly — to allow our self to develop, so that we eventually have the possibility of controlling sexual lust? This 'eventually' has now arrived! We have certainly developed sufficiently by now. And so it is time that the Church designed a different teaching with regard to the *motus inordinatus.* However, I do not think that the Church will undertake such action in the near future.

Conclusion

Through the history of Christianity, the Church has always been afraid of the *motus inordinatus.* Human lust is the cause of the Fall from Paradise. Humans who live by the flesh and not by the spirit will never find God. People in the mystic temples were already aware of this. That is the reason for celibacy. At the beginning of the Christian era, the mysteries became decadent resulting in orgies. Sex was therefore also regarded in the same category. The Church wanted to prevent this and thus ordered strict celibacy. At least, this was how those seeking God should live. This applied to men (priests and monks) and women (nuns).

9. Is the Church Misogynist?

The Priory believes that Constantine and his male
successors successfully converted the world from
matriarchal paganism to patriarchal Christianity by
waging a campaign of propaganda that demonized
the sacred feminine, obliteration the goddess from
modern religion forever.

The Da Vinci Code, Chapter 28

At home I have a beautiful Catholic statue of Mary with
the infant Jesus in her arms. Every time I dust Mary, I have
a word with her. Then I say things like 'What a world, eh,
Mary?' Not much more than that. My mother has a simple
Mary altar in her home, with a black Madonna. When my
father was dispatched to Indonesia as a soldier in 1946, he
gave my mother an ornamental tile with a picture of Mary as
Everlasting Comfort.

In 2004, the World Youth Days of the Catholic Church were
held on the Marienfeld in Cologne. A life-size icon of the
Virgin Mary, the mother of the Church, was carried around. In
1965, the Church declared the sinner Mary Magdalene holy.
Has the Church truly exiled the sacred feminine?

Not anti-feminine but anti-sex

It is not so much that the Church that has been anti-feminine,
but rather that the entire Western culture that has been anti-
feminine from the times of the Romans onward. When the
Roman Minucius Felix accused the Christians of performing
sexual rites, he said:

They recruit from the dregs of the population
nitwits and credulous women who solely by their
gender are unstable and easily influenced.[91]

This is abundantly clear. The entire Western culture was
patriarchal and the Church made a substantial contribution
to this. But the Church had also always been anti-macho in
terms of sexual lust. The man had to learn to control himself.
And because the culture was simply a patriarchal one, and the
woman was the 'object' of the male lust, the woman was the
great threat. This was the case as far back as the times of the
desert ascetic St Anthony (251–356). During his ascetic period
and solitude in the desert, the devil made repeated advances to
him, in all possible ways. One day the devil appeared to him
in the form of a beautiful woman:

He (the devil) whispered foul thoughts to him,
but Anthony drove him away with his prayers. He
attempted to excite him but as soon as Anthony
thought he might shame himself, he sheltered his
body behind faith and fasting. The miserable devil
even went as far as to appear one night as a woman, copying all her mannerisms for the sole purpose of seducing Anthony. But he thought of Christ
and the spiritual nobility of soul that we owe to
him, and he thus extinguished the glowing embers
of seduction.[92]

This is, as it were, the basic story that we consistently
encounter in the history of Christianity, as in the narrative of
the Grail knights, for example. They must live a celibate life,
but that is not easy when the devil is always eager to tempt
them, as happened to Perceval. One day, during one of his
many adventures, Perceval is rather depressed. He has lost his
horse, which is a grave matter for a knight, and falls asleep. He
wakes up in the middle of the night and a woman is standing in

front of him. She promises him a fine strong horse if he takes her into his service. Perceval believes that it is a woman who is addressing him, but in reality it is the enemy who wishes to deceive him to bring Perceval to 'that boundary where he will lose his soul forever.'[93] However, Perceval is willing to accept much as long as he can regain a horse — you're either a knight or you aren't! So he takes her into his service to give her support when she asks for it. When he has mounted his horse, the horse bolts off at full speed. Then Perceval understands that he has been deceived by the devil. He crosses himself, which causes the horse to stumble. The horse throws off his heavy load and disappears into a dark river.

Perceval comes out of this adventure unscathed, but further on in his exploits we find him under the influence of wine, overheated in bed with a young virgin. Just in time he sees his sword with the red cross engraved in it. This brings him to his senses. He crosses himself and the bed and the virgin vanishes. Our hero only just escaped breaking his oath of celibacy.

In contrast, Lancelot is not able to maintain his celibacy. In his case, it is not the devil that is responsible but the woman herself: Guinevere. For this reason, he will never be able to view the Grail.

Not only men are seduced by the devil. Merlin is the result of the union of his mother with the devil. The story runs as follows. The devils wish to create a man who is capable of undermining faith in Christ. For this purpose, they seek a very honourable and religious woman. They find one, but how can they seduce her? This is only possible if the woman gets into a rage and forgets Christ. This happens at the moment her sister — who makes herself available to all the young men — comes to visit her and complains about her righteous style of life. It is just a façade, her sister claims, after all, she has a relationship with her confessor. This is not true but the consequence is that the woman becomes extremely angry, and thus forgets Christ. When she falls asleep, the devil seizes his chance. He says:

'Now I can do with her what I like. She has forgotten the mercy of her Lord and the help of her
Masters and we can now take the opportunity to
generate our man in her.' Every devil who has the
possibility of joining with a woman was prepared
to do so. He came to the place where she slept and
lay with her. She woke up when she had been made
pregnant.[94]

Women, too, are not always capable — when they are asleep
— of controlling lust. At such times, the devil is also a threat
to them.

Reading about the disastrous fate of Lancelot is too much for
Francesca of Rimini and her lover Paolo. Dante mentions them
in his *Divine Comedy*. Francesca and her lover land in the second
ring of hell. Francesca explains to Dante what the cause of this
is. The story is set in Rimini in around 1275. Francesca has been
promised in marriage to Gianciotto. One day, she is reading with
Giancotto's brother, Paolo, about Lancelot and his yearnings:

One day, we were reading about Lancelot for our
pleasure and about his feelings of love. We were
alone, without really noticing it. The narrative
brought our gaze together more and more often
— and we turned pale. But one moment became
too much for us. When we read about how the
long awaited smile was so pleasantly kissed by the
lover — yes, that was when he who will never be
separated from me, greatly trembling, kissed my
mouth. That book was our Gallehault. We did not
read anymore that day.[95]

Man and woman come into hell as a consequence of corruption, this is what we read in Dante's lay literature. We can
learn something important from this. The writings in which
the man threatens to succumb to the seductions of the sinful

woman generally belong to the religiously oriented literature and cover monks and Grail knights. Otherwise it is lay literature in which man and woman are equally bad if they succumb to lust.

Abelarde and Heloise

Dante describes the tragic history of Francesca and Paolo at the beginning of the fourteenth century, but another renowned love story was known much earlier — that between Abelarde (1079–1142) and Heloise (1110–63). Abelarde was a famous scholar in Paris. This was the reason for the canon of Notre Dame in Paris, Fulbert, to ask him to become tutor to his niece, Heloise, in his home. Heloise was twenty years younger than Abelarde. Abelarde received free board and lodgings in Fulbert's house, for which he gave Heloise lessons in return. This was asking for trouble. A passionate love affair resulted. To cut a splendid but long story short, the love was discovered by Fulbert. In a fit of anger, he castrated Abelarde and Heloise landed in a cloister. They married because Heloise was pregnant. The poor child was given the name Pierre Astralabius. Abelarde and Heloise maintained contact. In one of her letters, Heloise asks Abelarde why the Benedictine cloister regulations appied equally to men and women, while women were so much weaker. The long response by Abelarde is remarkable — What do you mean, the weaker sex? Look at the women around Jesus! Are they not stronger than the Apostles who flee away from the crucifixion, while the women remain steadfast? And look at Mary Magdalene who Jesus allows to salve him — to make him king — which he does not allow anyone else. Then Abelarde writes:

> Try on these grounds to form an idea of the exceptional value of the woman. The living Christ was twice salved by a woman, both his feet and his head. He received the sacramental initiation

of a king and a priest from a woman. ... Salving
by the woman is an indication of his exceptional
rank in both his monarchy and his priesthood.
The salving on his head refers to the higher rank,
while that of the feet refers to the lower. Please
note that he accepts the sacramental royal salving from a woman, while he rejected the rule
offered to him by men and fled from them when
they wanted to take him and appoint him king
by force. The woman realized the initiation of a
heavenly king, not an earthly one. She initiated the
man who later said about himself: My kingdom is
not of this world. Archbishops glory when, under
loud acclaim from the people, they salve earthly
kings and when they initiate mortal priests, they
are wrapped in splendid robes with golden weave.
And nevertheless, they frequently bless the people
who curse the Lord! A simple woman completed
this sacrament for Christ. For this purpose she
had not put on other clothes, had not made herself
up, but nevertheless she performed this rite, to the
dissatisfaction of the disciples, not on the basis of
her function as a functionary but purely due to the
merits of her piety.[96]

Abelarde subsequently deals extensively with the deaconesses of the first centuries of Christianity. For example, he
quotes from the letters of Paul to Timothy, the challenged
letters, in which Paul says that women should not teach and
should keep silent at communal gatherings (1Tim.2:12). When
Paul speaks of 'real widows' (1Tim.5:5–10), Abelarde believes
that the reference is to deaconesses. These deaconesses played
a major role in early communities, as Paul indicates at the end
of his letter to the Romans in around AD 56. The ending is as
follows:

> I commend you to our sister Phoebe, a deaconess
> of the Church of Cenchreae, that you may receive
> her in the Lord as befits the saints, and help her
> in whatever she may require from you, for she
> has been a helper of many and of myself as well.
> Greet Prisca and Aquilla, my fellow workers in
> Jesus Christ, who risked their necks for my life.
> (Rom.16:1–3)

Abelarde goes with a fine-toothed comb through these kind of statements in the Scriptures, also those in the Old Testament. Female prophets are worth much more than male ones, including Isaiah, says Abelarde, because mercy works better in them.[97] Female martyrs are also worth more than male ones. Take, for example, the woman who is tortured with her seven sons in Maccabeans. Isn't that worth more than the martyr's death of Eleazar, the most prominent of the Scripture scholars (2Macc.6, 7)? Abelarde also goes through the scriptures of the Church Fathers in this way. he is actually a precursor of feminist theology, although he is not always seen in this way because he seduced poor Heloise.

It is thus interesting when Abelarde writes about the Church Fathers, because you can often read the works of the Church Fathers in two ways. One way demonstrates how anti-feminine they are, the other way is exactly the opposite. Abelarde does the latter. It is the story of the whore and the saint. When the Church Fathers are talking about the woman as a whore, they are actually talking about their own lust. But when they are talking about the woman as a saint, they are speaking of the honourable widows in Christ, and they are full of praise for these. Take, for example, the Church Father St Jerome (342–420), who was quoted by Abelarde to show how much he admired women. Particularly the Roman Paula and her family were praised by Paul. This true Christian founded a female community in Rome. He extols the honour of holy women. But, at the same time, St Jerome knows the experiences of the

enticement of young girls, of the devil, in fact. This is when
he is living as an ascetic in the Syrian desert. He discovers that
this is not the true Christian ideal, because you can live as an
ascetic until you weigh an ounce, 'nevertheless you are encir-
cled by groups of dancing girls time after time.'[98] It is not the
woman that represents evil, but one's own lust. That is what the
Church is afraid of.

Feminine emancipation in the Middle Ages: mysticism

The Church has always extolled saintly women. This is amply
demonstrated by medieval mysticism. If there is anywhere
in history where women exert influence on the Church and
the state, it is the female mystics who did so. Hildegard von
Bingen (1098–1179) had a great deal of influence. She accused
the German emperor Frederick Barbarossa in unequivocal
terms that he was causing too much friction with the pope:

> O King, it is urgently necessary that you are care-
> ful in your actions. I see you in a secret vision
> as a child, as a thoughtless living creature before
> the Living Eyes (of God). You still have time, to
> govern over earthly matters. Be careful that the
> Highest King does not cause you to fall due to the
> blindness of your eyes that do not see exactly how
> you should hold the sceptre of just rule in your
> hand. Therefore, beware: live in a way that the
> mercy of God does not extinguish in you.[99]

It must have been strange for an emperor to receive this kind
of letter from a woman. And yet he listened to her. The Pope
also did the same when he was living in exile in Avignon two
centuries later. The mystic Catherine of Siena herself went to
see the Pope in Avignon in 1376. She had previously written
to Pope Gregory in no mean terms:

> Dear Holy Father. The unworthy poor daughter
> in Christ appeals to you in his precious blood ...
> I would dearly like to see in you a male (virile)
> spirit, free of fear and egoism and free of worldly
> love for your family ... that is why my soul pas-
> sionately yearns that God in his mercy will remove
> your less benign traits and will form a new man
> from you with a fervent longing for reform. Other-
> wise, you will not be able to fulfil the will of God
> and the intimate longing of his servants. Forgive
> me, dear Father, my encouragement. But God, who
> is the Truth, compels me to say this.[100]

The Babylonian exile of the popes in Avignon — they did not have their seats in Rome but in Avignon between 1309 and 1377 — was a source of irritation to Catherine. All kinds of power games between the North Italian cities and the clergy were the cause of this. The pope is also impressed by the mystical depths of Catherine, as he is of the mystic Brigitta of Sweden who came to visit him. The pope asked Catherine to give a sign when he ought to depart for Rome. She wrote back that Christ had revealed to her that he should simply go. And he goes. Op 16 September 1376, the papal court departed toward Rome. Catherine also returned to Siena.

Conclusion

If we were to take Christian mysticism as the starting point for historiography, the woman would suddenly occupy a much more prominent place in history. Mysticism is full of free, proud and independent women who do not shrink from telling popes and emperors how to behave. And if we believe Abelarde, women are even stronger than men. The Church may have been less anti-feminine than people nowadays claim. It is more a matter of an anti-sex attitude. And this applies equally to the man.

10. The Blessed Mary and the Blessed Mary Magdalene

The early Church

There is not much friction in the first few centuries of the Christian era. The Church Fathers conjure up beautiful, grand and pious representations of the Virgin Mary. She is the second Eve, the Theotokos (Mother of God), the servant to the Lord, the strong-willed woman, the leader of the heavenly choir, model of chastity and Blessed Mother, Mater Gloriosa and the sacred feminine. She is Queen of the Heavens and our refuge in good and bad times. And much more.

With regard to Mary Magdalene, there was not much controversy in the first few centuries. The Church Fathers still referred to her as the 'Apostolic Apostolorum,' the apostle of the apostles. In Gnostic and ecclesiastical Christian circles she was honoured as the first to have seen the resurrected Jesus. Mary Magdalene was not yet regarded as the Mary from whom Jesus exorcised seven demons. Jesus exorcised 'seven spirits' from Martha's sister (Luke 8:2), but we do not know if this was the same Mary that Jesus saw after the crucifixion. The idea that it was the same Mary only arose in the sixth century when Gregory the Great (Pope from 590 to 604) linked both Marys together. He did so on the basis of a third Mary; the one who dries Jesus's feet with her hair and salves him in Luke 7:3. Luke says of this Mary that she was known in the town as a 'sinner.' But we do not know if this is the same Mary from whom Jesus exorcises the spirits, or if it is the same one who first sees Jesus after the resurrection. To Gregory, this was not a problem; they were all the same Mary. Why he made this choice remains a mystery. Whatever the case, it was an easy interpretation. In this way, a one-dimensional picture of Mary Magdalene was generated: she was a sinful woman (a prostitute) who was converted, became one of Jesus's most faithful followers, dried Jesus's feet with her hair, salved him and was the first to see him after the resurrection. It is the ideal image of a conversion. This was probably Gregory's intention. This is the way she has been viewed in the Christian tradition ever since.

Mary and Mary Magdalene in the Middle Ages

The worship of Mary really began to flourish in the twelfth century, when the cult of the Virgin Mary arose. The great initiator of this movement was no less than Bernard of Clairvaux, whom we have encountered previously. He elucidated his ideas in four sermons, when still a young man of around twenty-five years old. In his sermons he said, among other things:

> For this reason, loving Virgin, the distressed Adam, exiled from paradise with his unfortunately descendants, begs you; for this reason Abraham begs you; for this reason, David begs you; for this reason the holy arch-fathers beg you, your own forefathers who now inhabit the land of the shadow of death. The entire world expects this of you, bowing at your knees, and not unjustly for the consolation of the miserable, the liberation of the prisoners, the salvation of the condemned, and finally the welfare of all of Adam's children, that is, of all your children, depends on you. Give us your answer soon, O Virgin. Speak the word that the Earth, underworld, and heaven expect, O Queen.[101]

Mary, the Mother of God, is the intercessor for all humans. 'O Queen,' Bernard called out on numerous occasions in these four sermons. Mary was not only a Virgin: she was also fertile. She was the fertile Virgin, Mother of all life.

This is also more or less what happens to Mary Magdalene. Although Pope Gregory may have represented her as a converted prostitute, this did not stop her from being extremely popular in he Middle Ages. For example, the Archbishop of Mainz and the Abbot Rabanus Maurus (776–856), of the renowned monastery of Fulda, wrote a monumental work on the life of Mary Magdalene. As with the Virgin Mary, the popularity of Mary Magdalene grew enormously in the twelfth century. In his sermons on the Song of Songs, Bernard of Clairvaux even referred to her as 'the bride of Christ.' This is certainly the Mary who was the sister of Martha. And in doing so, Bernard meant the 'spiritual bride:'

> We even have the reflective Mary in those who,
> after some time, with the aid of God's mercy,
> have managed to reach something better and
> more fortunate because, trusting in forgiveness,
> they are no longer oppressed by the sad picture
> of their sins but rather find an insatiable pleasure
> in considering God's rule day and night, where
> with uncovered countenance they occasionally
> reflect the glory of the Bridegroom with unutter-
> able joy.[102]

Bernard did not place the emphasis on the sins but rather on the victory over sin in mystic exercises. In every mystic lurks a Mary, as it were, who can view the bridegroom with uncovered countenance.

Mary Magdalene and Modern Devotion

In the Modern Devotion Movement people are not as positive as Bernard was. In this movement, the accent was placed upon sinfulness. The Modern Devotion Movement was founded by Geert Groote (1340–84) from the Low Countries. Groote was a student of the mystic Jan van Ruusbroec

(1293–1381), but in contrast to Ruusbroec, Groote did not seek mystic experiences but rather a lifestyle of devotion. The standard work of the movement is the *Imitatio Christi* by Thomas à Kempis (*c.* 1380–1471). After the Bible, this is the most translated book in the world. The essential message actually issues from the title — the imitation of Christ's lifestyle. The brothers and (many) sisters from 'the movement of the brothers and sisters of ordinary life,' as the movement is often called, pursue a life of simplicity, sobriety and strict self-knowledge. There are frequent references to our sinful condition. It is no surprise that the life of Mary Magdalene is cited as an example. In the *Imitatio Christi,* she is one of the few saints who are mentioned. That is also logical, because the book is about a direct relationship with Jesus; saints are no longer needed as intermediaries. It can be expressed as follows: as a result of two centuries of mysticism, Jesus Christ can now be experienced in our hearts. He can be found there. The followers of Modern Devotion seek him there. But one first has to go through one's own sinful state, just like Mary Magdalene did. The *Imitatio Christi* contains the following passage:

> When Jesus is with us, everything is good, and
> nothing seems difficult. But if Jesus is not with us,
> everything is so hard. If Jesus does not speak to us
> in our innermost soul, all consolation is so poor.
> But if Jesus speaks a single word, one experiences
> this as a rich comfort. Didn't Mary Magdalene
> stand at the place where she cried when Martha
> said to her: the Master is there, and he calls you.[103]

And:

> O dear Lord Jesus! How rich is the pleasure of the
> God-loving soul, which participates in your meal
> with you, where no other food is given but you

> yourself, its only love, desirable above everything
> that a heart can desire! It should also be possible
> for me to cry in your presence of intimate love
> and to spray your feet with tears like the pious
> Magdalene.[104]

The practice was formed around these thoughts, by the devoted nun Alijt Bake (1415–55), in the Galilee cloister in Ghent. Alijt Bake read mystic scriptures and was very devout, which led to mystical experiences, not in emulation of Jesus but rather of Mary Magdalene. She wrote in her autobiography, *My Beginning and Progress:*

> I wished nothing else but to lie at his feet, along
> with Mary Magdalene. That is why I sought the
> solitude of the cloister.[105]

It may have been better for her not to do so, for it only led to envy on the part of the other nuns. She had mystical experiences in this solitude and the others did not accept this. After all, it was quite haughty that a sinful soul had a direct relationship with Jesus. Alijt was known as a rather independent and rebellious nun, which led to a number of conflicts. She said that she would be mad to follow the paths of the other sisters. She wrote that 'While I am almost at the top of the tower, the sisters ask me to come down and to use their ladder.' Ultimately, she managed to reach a compromise, the conflicts were resolved and she even became the prioress of the cloister. But the damage had been done. The congregation of the district chapter intervened, she was exiled from the cloister in 1455, and the chapter forbade women writing and copying mystic and philosophical works. It was only around this time that a negative view of women arose in the Church.

Mary and the Protestant churches

Luther (1483–1546) and particularly Calvin (1506–64) found fertile ground for their teachings in northern Europe. Modern Devotion paved the way for Calvin, as it did not make much effort to accommodate women, who tended to be involved in all kinds of mysticism. Calvinism represented the upsurge of masculine rational thought. Calvin rejected the worship of saints. In his *Institution,* he wrote of the cursed papist practice of the intercession of the Virgin Mary:

> How and with which pretext can they defend ...
> that they worship the holy Virgin because they re-
> quest her to order her Son to do what they demand
> and desire.[106]

In the Catholic Church it is common practice to ask Mary, not Jesus, to intercede with God. Jesus is not directly addressed. Mary is the *mediatrix,* the intermediary. You might even wonder whether Mary is addressed more than Jesus himself. During the Reformation, people rejected this custom. After the Modern Devotion Movement, Jesus Christ himself became the focal point. The emphasis was on the direct relationship between the believer and Jesus, and no intermediary was necessary. The worship of Mary — and other saints — was regarded as idolatry. In 1523, one of the leaders of the Reformatio, Ulrich Zwingli, wrote:

> Because Christ is the only intercessor between God
> and us, there are no other intermediaries needed
> after this life than he.[107]

The Reformation was primarily concerned with *solus Christus,* only Christ, and *sola Scriptura,* only the Scriptures.

Modern worship of Mary

For the worship of the Holy Virgin, the Mother of God, we
have to go to the Catholic Church, and anyone who thinks
this is mere popular piety has it by the wrong end. During the
Second Vatican Council of 1962–64, the Veneration of Mary
was re-established in the Catholic Church. The appropriate text
is as follows:

> The Virgin Mary, who at the message of the angel
> received the Word of God in her heart and in her
> body and gave Life to the world, is acknowledged
> and honoured as being truly the Mother of God and
> Mother of the Redeemer. Redeemed by reason of
> the merits of her Son and united to him by a close
> and indissoluble tie, she is endowed with the high
> office and dignity of being the Mother of the Son
> of God, by which account she is also the beloved
> daughter of the Father and the temple of the Holy
> Spirit. Because of this gift of sublime grace she
> far surpasses all creatures, both in heaven and on
> earth. ... The Catholic Church, taught by the Holy
> Spirit, honours her with filial affection and piety as
> a most beloved mother.
>
> Wherefore this Holy Synod, in expounding
> the doctrine on the Church, in which the divine
> Redeemer works salvation, intends to describe with
> diligence both the role of the Blessed Virgin in the
> mystery of the Incarnate Word and the Mystical
> Body, and the duties of redeemed mankind toward
> the Mother of God, who is mother of Christ and
> mother of men, particularly of the faithful ...
>
> Taken up to heaven she did not lay aside this
> salving duty, but by her constant intercession con-
> tinued to bring us the gifts of eternal salvation. By
> her maternal charity, she cares for the brethren of

her Son, who still journey on earth surrounded by dangers and cultics, until they are led into the happiness of their true home. Therefore the Blessed Virgin is invoked by the Church under the titles of Advocate, Auxiliatrix, Adjutrix, and Mediatrix. This, however, is to be so understood that it neither takes away from nor adds anything to the dignity and efficaciousness of Christ the one Mediator.[108]

And this only referred to the veneration of Mary in the Western Catholic Church. Mary as Theokotos, the Mother of God, may even have a more prominent place in the Greek Orthodox Church than in the Catholic Church. In Greek Orthodox circles, Mary is honoured as the Holy Sophia, Hagia Sophia. There is also the veneration of Sophia in the Russian Orthodox Church, by Russian writers and by the Protestant mystic, Jakob Böhme (see Chapter 2). There is even the worship of Mary in Islam. The Koran states: 'Mary was chosen by God above all women in the world.' (Sura 3.42)

And, in the Catholic Church, Mary Magdalene is represented as a prostitute as often as she is characterized as a saint. The fact that today Mary Magdalene is being 'rediscovered' in Protestant theology seems to be a typically Protestant approach.[109] In the Catholic Church Mary and Mary Magdalene have never been away, although they may have been disregarded, especially by nineteenth-century theology, which was a very masculine and rational culture. Theodor Ritschl (1822–89), the theological professor, wrote on Catholic mysticism and Protestant piety that: 'this is a dotingly emasculated lifestyle.' Of course, a veneration of Mary does not fit in with this.

Conclusion

The Virgin Mary, Mother of God, never truly disappeared from the echelons of the Catholic Church. She may even receive more supplications than Jesus Christ or God himself. Mary is a constant in the Catholic faith. This is less so with Mary Magdalene. Until deep in the Middle Ages she was generally regarded as the first of the apostles. It was only in the late Middle Ages that the Modern Devotion Movement began to place the emphasis on the sinner; the converted prostitute. But even in the Modern Devotion Movement, mystical women such as Alijt Bake took Mary Magdalene as an example. The worship of Mary and Mary Magdalene declined during the Reformation. In the masculine rational theology of the nineteenth century, Mary and Mary Magdalene tended to disappear from view, but they never truly vanished from the Catholic Church.

11. Why Jesus Was Not Married

'Moreover, Jesus as a married man makes infinitely
more sense than our standard biblical view of Jesus as
a bachelor.'
'Why?' Sophie asked.
'Because Jesus was a Jew,' Langdon said, ... 'and the
social decorum during that time virtually forbade a Jewish man to be unmarried. According to Jewish custom,
celibacy was condemned ...'

The Da Vinci Code, Chapter 58.

In the previous chapters, sufficient arguments have been made
to show that there was no convincing reason why Jesus should
have been married to Mary Magdalene.

In Chapters 1 and 2, I showed that the 'kiss' of Jesus and
Mary Magdalene referred to an initiation rite and not a love
affair. In Chapter 3, I demonstrated that the secret of the Grail
referred to the meeting of the Resurrected Christ and not to the
physical blood line of Jesus and Mary Magdalene. In Chapters 5
and 6 I discussed the problem of dual-nature theology, which is
a problem that has dominated the whole of Christian history.

The notion of Dan Brown that Jesus was a man (and not
God) is a unilateral materialist approach and not esoteric at all.
In Chapter 7, I recounted that it was extremely improbable that
the Knights Templar practised sexual rites. Dan Brown probably took his inspiration from the Ordo Templi Oriento from
the beginning of the twentieth century.

Finally, in Chapters 9 and 10, I illustrated that the Church has
not been anti-feminine all these years, although it has disparaged
sex. If there is anywhere in the patriarchal culture of the West
where the feminine has been championed, it has probably been

the Catholic Church with its veneration of the Virgin Mary and Mary Magdalene. There may have been a historical reason why the Church has been anti-sex all this time.

In this closing chapter, I wish to examine the historical arguments why Jesus was not married to Mary Magdalene. Like a good number of esoteric proponents of a marriage between Jesus and Mary Magdalene, Dan Brown also uses the argument that is was extremely unusual for Jewish men not to be married at the time of Jesus. Is that really true? We shall provide a few examples.

John the Baptist, the Essenes, and other Jewish holy men

Is it likely that John the Baptist, who ate locusts and wore camel-hair clothes, was married? Probably not. Whatever the case may be, he certainly did not live according to Jewish customs. So, it would seem unlikely that he was married.

Who was John the Baptist? Was he a lonely soul, calling out in the desert, or did he belong to a Jewish sect? This question has been studied comprehensively by historians, and the general conclusion is that he belonged to the Jewish sect called the 'baptists.' They were probably a group of Jews of which the present-day Mandeans in Southern Iraq are distant descendants. Some of ancient Mandeans texts have survived. Another ancient Jewish baptismal sect is that of the Elchasaites; the baptist sect in which Mani was raised in the vicinity of modern-day Baghdad. Mani preached celibacy for the Manichaean *electi,* who were both men and women. This was also the case for Mandaean priests, and the priestesses of the Elchasaites. The surviving Mandaean texts display a strong antipathy to Jewish temple rites, which was perhaps the reason why the baptismal sect lived initially in the trans-Jordanian desert, and moved to the Babylonian empire in around AD 30, eventually settling in the south. Their hero was John the Baptist, not Jesus. The Mandeans upheld a strong dualism. The earthly life was experienced as a prison and the followers looked forward to the coming of the Messiah. Thus, the Mandeans were Jewish Gnostics, perhaps a branch of the Essenes. They were also referred to as the Nazarenes, just like Jesus, in fact. A kinship between the Mandeans and the Gospel of John was alleged.

One of the Mandaean texts deals with John the Baptist, called 'Yahya' here. The text indicates his complete renunciation of worldly things and his celibate lifestyle as an ideal for the Mandaean priests:

> Yahya preached in the nights and said: 'By the actions of my Father I give light and by praise of the Man, my creator, I have freed my soul of the world and of the works that are hateful and evil ... I stand in the strength of my Father and with the praise of the Man, my creator. I have not built a house in Judea, I have not placed a throne in Jerusalem. I have not loved the garland of roses. I have not had union with amorous women. I have not loved weakness nor have I enjoyed the cup of the drunkards. I have not rejoiced in food for the body and evil has found no place in me. I have not forsaken my evening prayers, neither have I forgotten the mighty Jordan. I have not forgotten my baptisms.[110]

The baptist Jewish sects thus engaged in a strong renunciation of the world. To reiterate Paul once again: the celibacy for the priest-initiate fitted in well with this approach.

The Essenes

The Essenes were a kindred Jewish sect at the time of Jesus. Nowadays they are famous for the Dead Sea Scrolls that were found in 1948. The Essenes were Jewish and certainly not Christians, even although some kind of kinship can be demonstrated. According to many modern books, Jesus may have been an Essene. The Essenes also had a strong antipathy to temple practices. The priests were apparently over-Hellenized and had strayed too far from the true Jewish faith. This antipathy was not shared by Jesus. He regularly visited the Temple, even although he too occasionally thought that worldly matters occupied a too-dominant position. He is well-known for overturning the tables of the money-lenders.

It has now been established that the Essenes learned to be celibate. At least, that was the case with their priests. We know this from the Jewish history of Flavius Josephus (c. AD 37–100/110), in which he writes of the Essenes:

> They are Jewish by birth but maintain much more friendly relationships with one another than the others. They avoid pleasure as if it were a sin, and regard modesty and the suppression of passion as a virtue. They abhor marriage but they adopt other people's children who are receptive to their teachings. They absorb them into their circles and form them according to their own principles. They do not condemn marriage and having children, but they protect themselves against female licentiousness and they are convinced that no single woman remains faithful to a man.[111]

Just as with the Mandeans, celibacy for the priests was a logical consequence of their dualist view of the world.

Other Jewish holy men

Around AD 120, Rabbi Simeon ben Azzai travelled through the Jewish countryside. We know him from the many quoted passages on the danger of mystic speculations. The narrative is as follows. The rabbis, Simeon ben Azzai, Simeon ben Zoma and Aqiba, are in a state of ecstasy. At a certain moment, Rabbi

Aqiba warns the others: 'When you have arrived at the stones of pure marble, do not say: "Water! Water!" because it has been said: He who tells lies cannot stand in front of my eyes' (Psalms 101:7). Rabbi ben Azzai looked and died; Simeon ben Zoma looked and was struck by madness; Rabbi Aqiba left in peace.[112] In the *Tosefta*, Rabbi ben Azzai and Rabbi Eleazer are talking to one another about sexual reproduction:

> Rabbi Simeon ben Azzai spoke: 'He who does not participate in reproduction is acting against the Scriptures and destroys the image of God. For it has been said: "God created man in his own image" and "go forth and multiply" (Gen.1:27f).'
> Rabbi Eleazar said to him: 'Fine words come from the mouth of the one who does this [acting against the Scriptures]. A man interprets well and acts well: Ben Azzai interprets well but he does not act well!' Rabbi Simeon ben Azzai said to him: 'What must I do? My soul thirsts for the Torah. The maintenance of the world is in the hands of others.'[113]

Simeon ben Azzai lives for the Torah, not for the maintenance of the world. Apparently he has no time for things other than a study of the Torah, and although that is condemned by Rabbi Eleazar, it evidently does occur among Rabbis who engage in mysticism.

Conclusion

These are just a few examples that illustrate that serious God-seekers in ancient Jewry were celibate. Baptist sects, Essenes, and some rabbis were examples of this. The idea that Jewry does not acknowledge celibacy is not true. Jesus allowed himself to be baptized by John the Baptist. So it is probable that he, too, was celibate. After all, he was the greatest God-seeker of them all.

12. A Short History of Esoteric Christianity

Terminology

According to Webster, 'esoteric' means 'with a meaning that is understood only by those who have received the necessary instruction / with a private or secret meaning or purpose.' Thus, esoteric Christianity deals with the secrets of Christianity. Usually, the concept of esoteric Christianity is contrasted with the notion of *exoteric* Christianity, which refers to the Church and tradition. Esoteric Christianity is thus extra-ecclesiastical Christianity; Gnosticism, Manichaeism, Catharism, Rosicrucians, and anthroposophy, for example. They are Christian movements that refer to Gnosis to arrive at an insight into, and an experience of, God. The twentieth-century findings in the Nag Hammadi library and the many Manichaean scriptures have ensured that esoteric Christianity is no longer 'secret.' However, it is not correct to place all forms of extra-ecclesiastical Christianity under one denominator. For example, ancient Gnosis and medieval Cathars teach Docetism, whereas mysticism and anthroposophy teach crucifixion and resurrection. Just as there are many 'churches' in traditional Christianity, there are also many variants of so-called 'esoteric Christianity.'

Besides the umbrella significance, the term 'esoteric Christianity' also has a more refined meaning. It refers to the Christian movements that take as their basis a triple relationship involving Being. The relationship is: God — cosmos/nature — mankind.

In these Christian movements, it is assumed that God is the transcendent (God is far away), is pantheistic (God is simultaneously present in creation), and is immanent (God is in the soul). This triple image of God is elaborated in alchemy,

109

particularly the natural philosophy movement of seventeenth-
and eighteenth-century Germany — also called 'radical pietism.' The search for the Philosopher's Stone, or the *quinta
essential,* or the means to turn lead into gold is actually the
search for the current presence of Christ in Creation. To discover this secret, one has to be a mystic, scientist and theologist. This combination was quite common in the seventeenth
and eighteenth centuries.

This narrow concept of esoteric Christianity can
include Manichaeism, seventeenth- and eighteenth-century
Rosicrucians as well as modern anthroposophy, but not
ancient Gnosticism, the Cathars or many New Age groups.

The Gnostics and the Cathars taught vertical dualism, meaning that everything above is good and everything below is evil.
Creation was realized by an evil demi-urge, often equated
with Yahweh. By contrast, in the New Age movement, people
tend to cherish exclusively the immanent image of God. God
corresponds to Creation and the soul. People can thus become
God themselves. This has always been denied by natural philosophy, in which God always remains the Other.

Natural philosophy has not always been outside traditional
Christianity. Johann Valentin Andreae (1586–1654, the author
of the 'Rosicrucian scripts' in 1614–16) was originally a
Lutheran preacher, and Jakob Böhme was an extremely devout
pietist, a mystic in fact. Nevertheless, he ended up outside the
Church. It is a different story in medieval mysticism. Mysticism
was the internal search for God. Christian mysticism flourished from around 1100 to around 1400, with a few offshoots
in Spain (Teresa of Avila and John of the Cross). Mysticism
was characterized by the dual relationship: God and mankind,
as was always the case in ecclesiastical Christianity. In this,
Christianity is related to Gnosticism and Catharism — albeit in
a moderate form. All kinds of lateral connections can be found
between so-called esoteric and so-called exoteric Christianity.

In this book, I understand esoteric Christianity to be those
forms of Christianity that take as their starting point:

1. the possibility that the soul can develop to higher forms of knowledge and experience, as in Gnosticism and mysticism;

2. the possibility that substance can turn into spirit and vice versa, as in the case of Catholic transubstantiation and alchemy;

3. as an extension to this, those Christian groups that accept the incarnation of God, the crucifixion and the resurrection.

According to this definition, ancient Gnosticism is not esoteric Christianity (although it is Gnostic Christianity) because it rejects the crucifixion and resurrection. The same applies to the Cathars. Mysticism is not esoteric Christianity because mysticism denies the possibility that substance can undergo a process of transubstantiation (except in the Eucharist). Traditional Christianity is not esoteric Christianity because it (currently) denies the development into higher forms of perception, as well as transubstantiation of matter. But the Church does teach the crucifixion and resurrection. I believe that these three criteria are also met in Manichaeism, moderate forms of Gnosticism, natural philosophy (Rosicrucians and alchemists), and in anthroposophy. To eliminate misunderstanding: all development on the path to higher forms of knowledge begins with respect, devotion and belief. As is stated in the Benedictine rule for monks: the exercises in humility are the first step. Anyone who skips this step is acting out of pride.

Esoteric Christianity in the first few centuries

Esoteric Christianity — according to the above-mentioned definition — was propagated in the first few centuries of Christianity by Valentinus (c.100–160), by Origen (185–254), by a splendid but difficult text entitled *Pistis Sophia* (Wisdom of Faith) as well as by a text entitled *De Ascencio Iesaia* (The Ascension of Isaiah), and also by the Manichaeans.

We know Valentinus from his work *The Gospel of Truth.*
Gilles Quispel referred to him as the greatest Gnostic of antiquity. This was not Gnosticism but Gnosis! Valentinus studied in
Alexandria where he came into contact with the new phenomenon of Christianity. When he became a Christian, he departed
for Rome, but his Christianity was certainly not the Christianity
of the later Catholics. People believe that he belonged to the
Christian sect of the *Gnóstikoi.* In this sect, people identified the
divine *Anthropos* with the eternal Christ from the Gospel of John.
Just like many Gnostic groups, Valentinus also distinguished
between the evil demiurge-Creator and the Unknown God who
had nothing to do with Creation. But in contrast to the Gnostics,
Valentinus does not teach Docetism. To Valentinus, it was certainly the Anthropos-Christ who died and was resurrected. This
is what he wrote in *The Gospel of Truth.*

> This is why the merciful and faithful-one —
> Yeshua! — patiently endured the sufferings ...
> since he knew that his death is life for many ... He
> was nailed to a crossbeam in order to publish the
> edict of the Father on the cross. O sublime teach-
> ing, such that he humbled himself unto death while
> clad in eternal life! He stripped off the rags of
> mortality in order to don this imperishability which
> none has the power to take from him.[114]

This leaves little to the imagination. For the rest, the *Gospel
of Truth,* and other writings by Valentinus, are characterized
by a complicated cosmological system that describes how the
Anthropos descended through the many heavenly realms to
the earth.

This descent — and ascent — is splendidly described in *De
Ascencio Iesaia,* an anonymous text that originated in Jewish-
esoteric circles but was Christianized in the third century. This
work describes how the prophet Isaiah ascended through the
heavenly realms and, having arrived at the Father in the seventh

realm, saw how Christ descends to the earth. When Christ passed the various realms the angels in those realms did not recognize Christ as such because he was dressed consistently in the cloak of the relevant angelic hierarchy. Having arrived on earth he assumed the fleshly cloak of mankind, and died on the cross to be resurrected in a glorious body. In that body he made a return journey through the heavenly spheres but now all the angels saw him in his divine state and sang 'Sanctus, Sanctus, Sanctus.'

All this is described, in a different way of course, in the anonymous Gnostic text entitled *Pistis Sophia,* which opens with the sentence:

> It came to pass, when Jesus had risen from the
> dead, that he passed eleven years discoursing with
> his disciples.[115]

There is no possible misunderstanding, the main character — sometimes called Jesus, sometimes the First Mystery and sometimes the Saviour — must be the resurrected Jesus. For eleven years Jesus teaches his disciples about his divine origins and assignment. It is a story full of aeons and emanations.

The Church Father, Origen of Alexandria, also devoted much Gnostic attention to pre-existence, and also to that of the human soul. Not only did Jesus have a pre-nativity life, every person has that. This was a general belief in the first few centuries of Christianity. Later, in the sixth century, the teachings of Origen on the pre-existence of the soul were condemned by the Church.

It is difficult to say whether Origen was a Gnostic or a mystic. He was certainly a mystic when he developed the mysticism of the bride. To Origen, the pre-existent Logos could ultimately be found in the human soul due to the crucifixion and the resurrection. The human soul was the bride who entered into marriage with the bridegroom in the *hememonikón*. By this, Origen referred to the innermost soul where Christ could be found.

Augustine would later follow him in this, but without the element of pre-existence. Augustine was familiar with Gnosis in the form of Manichaeism, but to Augustine, a kind of pre-existent God-eclipse took place. He stated that God could only be found in the Scriptures.[116] And that he could be experienced in one's heart:

> See there he is, where truth is loved. He is within
> the very heart, yet hath the heart strayed from him.
> Go back into your heart, ye transgressors, and
> cleave fast to him that made you.[117]

With Augustine, there came an end to the 'Gnostic experience of life' in the first few centuries of Christianity. In other words, it was quite easy to look into the spiritual world in these first few centuries. This capacity gradually decreased and eventually vanished altogether. The way in which God became a man in Christ was no longer visible. The way Christ descended from the heavenly realms to assume a human form could no longer be perceived. What remained? The belief in the creed, the *credo*.

The Christian *credo* can be regarded as an ultimate summary of what people perceived in Gnostic circles in the first few centuries of Christianity. Much old Gnostic wisdom is contained in the creed. By this I mean esoteric wisdom according to the above-mentioned descriptions. What later became the ecclesiastic Christianity of Augustine said, right from the beginning, the pre-existence of Christ and mankind no longer interests us. He can be found here, on earth and in us. He can be found here; we must seek him here, not in distant heavens. This has been the central mission of the churches; to refer us to this single earthly life. Reincarnation does not fit in with this worldview. In the first few centuries of Christianity, people did know about the reincarnating soul, but the Church believed that this referred too much to pre-existence. We should not seek our identity here, we should seek it on earth. It is *here* that we have to become human. This led to the loss of much old truth and wisdom ... Yes, that is all part of evolution.

Esoteric Christianity in the Middle Ages

In his last year of life in North Africa, Augustine saw the approach of the Vandals. He must have realized that this represented the end of an era. The young Christian Church, which had just 'won' the struggle against the Gnostic Christians, and had just become the official state religion, was confronted with a new problem: that of the heathen Germans. It took around six centuries for the Church to convert the Germans to Christianity. There was not much scope for esoteric Christianity in this process, at least, not in Western Christianity. In Eastern Christianity, it was slightly different. The Eastern Roman Empire continued until 1435, when Byzantium was conquered by the Turks.

In the Western Church, it was only around the middle of the eleventh century that scope for a theological consideration of Christianity appeared. Scholasticism, mysticism, Catharism and Grail literature were all consequences of this.

In Scholasticism, people attempted to find God by means of reason. Anselm (1033–1109) and Thomas Aquinas (1225–74) developed the so-called 'proof of God.' This means that they tried by means of reason to prove that God exists — of course, they were certain of this — but they attempted to follow God's thought by means of reasoned argument. The question is: Can the reasoning of God be emulated? Anselm thought that this was possible, Thomas Aquinas was much less certain about this. In the last few years of his life, he discovered that this was *not* possible. He had a mystical experience which enabled him to experience God. In other words, God did not display Himself in reasoning but in experience. Disenchanted, Thomas then cried out: Everything I have done until now is straw!

People that were engaged in medieval mysticism knew for quite some time that God could not be approached via reason.

115

Bernard of Clairvaux, the inaugurator of medieval mysticism, has been comprehensively covered in previous chapters of this book. Bernard regarded the soul-capacity of the *memoria* as the instrument to open one's heart to God. In the next generation, adapted desire, *passion* are the motivating forces towards God, as is the case with the Flemish mystic, Hadewych. But *passion* has to be kept in check by reason. Reason alone does not give a desire for God, according to Hadewych:

> Reason has more sense of proportion than passion
> but passion knows the sweetness of sanctity more
> than reason. Nevertheless, these two help one an-
> other considerably, for reason educates passion and
> passion enlightens reason. When reason surrenders
> to the desire of passion and passion is tempered
> by the reaches of reason, they are capable of doing
> something exceptionally grand, and no one can
> learn this without feeling it.[118]

A generation later, Jan van Ruusbroec (1293–1381) confirmed this. In his *Ghierheit der Gheestelike Brulocht* (Yearning for Spiritual Marriage) he gives an expert description of the soul's journey toward God in three stages: the stage of the flesh, which he calls the 'working life;' the stage of the soul, which he calls the 'God-longing life;' and the finally the stage of the spirit, which he calls the 'God-see-ing life.' One can only get to know God by means of purely spiritual capacities.

In the whole of medieval mysticism, the quest was to find the ultimate union between (the soul of) man and God. Nature and the cosmos were not involved in this formula. However, Ruusbroec did see a relationship between the microcosm and the macrocosm. Just as man consists of three parts — body, mind and spirit — so the macrocosm consists of three heavens: the purely spiritual heaven of God; the firmament (stars and planets); and the lower heavenly realm (the ether and the earth), including the physical body of mankind. But it is a comparison; the three heavenly realms are symbolic of our spiritual life:

> All creatures show and teach us how we should live. The heavenly bodies and the system in which God placed them are to us an example and a true symbol of the way in which we must experience God above all elements of the heavens, by means of an internal and hidden spiritual life that no one knows or feels other than the one who experiences it, practises it, and maintains it.[119]

That there is a kinship between mankind and the three heavenly realms was normal medieval knowledge. It was not esoteric. Only getting to know God was 'internal and hidden.' This was also quite logical because the medieval citizen did not see God as being active in the cosmos or in nature. God was only active in the human soul. The idea that God was also active in the cosmos/nature was something that arose in seventeenth and eighteenth-century natural philosophy.

At the same time that medieval mysticism flourished, the rise and fall of the Cathars occurred in southern France. The Cathars were Gnostics. I dealt with them in Chapter 4, where I indicated that the Cathars sought God in the heavenly realms. Where Scholasticism sought God in reason, and mysticism sought God in the human heart, the Cathars sought God in the heavenly realms. All three cherished the idea that God could not be found in the cosmos/nature, but only in the relationship between God and mankind. The Cathars emphasized this dualism; the cosmos/nature was created by an evil demiurge.

The Cathars were consistent in their beliefs: they also denied the incarnation of Christ, the crucifixion and the resurrection. The adherents of mysticism and Scholasticism did not support these ideas. The mystics and the Cathars did overlap in that they both relied on the development into higher forms of human powers of knowledge: the Cathars achieved this with the help of Gnosis and the mystics with the help of *passion*. If we consider the aforementioned description of esoteric Christianity as a criterion, we must conclude that only mysticism was a form of esoteric Christianity. It was a weak form because mysticism only recognized the transubstantiation of the body and blood of Christ in the Eucharist, but not in substance as such. The latter is not important.

In the Middle Ages, there was only one 'school' in which people assumed that the divine was also to be found in nature. That was the cathedral School in Chartres. One of the magisters at this school was Bernardus Silvestris. His *Cosmographia* deals with the relationship between the microcosm and the macrocosm. The stars and planets are described as mythical figures. Even Creation is allocated a form with the name *Natura*. With this standpoint, the School of Chartres was rather unique, because it (almost) placed nature as a third principle between God and mankind. Contemporaries were not slow in offering criticism of these ideas. To most educated medieval citizens, Creation/nature was the 'book of nature;' the book that tells about God, rather than a subject of its own. The 'cosmologists,' as Bernardus Silvestris and his followers were called, thus assigned a different significance to nature. Silvestris wrote about this is his *Cosmographia*.

Just before Creation, *Natura* was in tears and said to *Noys,* which is God's providence or wisdom, that she was crying because of the deplorable state of primal matter, *hyle*. So *Noys* began to create. First of all, she (the wisdom of God) separated the four elements, then she placed the nine choirs of angels, the twelve signs of the zodiac and the other stars in the firmament, then the seven moving planets, the four winds (the ether), and finally the creation of the earth including, vegetables, grains, herbs, and trees. Then she begins on mankind. On the instructions of *Noys, Natura* goes looking for *Urania,* queen of the stars, and for *Physis,* who remains deep in the earth. *Natura* ascends through the heavenly spheres and finds *Urania*. Together they descend through the spheres to the earth. In the meantime they attempt to avoid the various (negative) influences of the planets. They eventually find *Physis* and they jointly create mankind. When they arrive in the highest heaven, *Urania* explains to *Natura* the intention of this marvellous story:

> Every virtue of the stars, every power in the firma-
> ment, every vitality that is found in the extremities
> of the heavens, every potentiality that is in the rays
> of those two shining bodies (sun and moon), and
> the five planets, let these things be know to her (the
> soul) when she enters the vehicle of her body.[120]

So mankind is seen as a microcosm, the stars and powers of the firmament are lodged in the soul of mankind. Bernardus Silvestris took this idea from Plato's *Timaeus* and the hermetic document, the *Asclepius*. The *Asclepius* was the only hermetic text known in the Middle Ages.

Esoteric Christianity in the New Age

The cathedral School of Chartres was an exception. Medieval mysticism began to decline around the mid-fourteenth century. The Cathars were exterminated around 1350. Scholasticism reached the definitive conclusion that God could not be known by means of reasoning. It was a matter of faith. The climate was no longer favourable for esoteric Christianity and a new impulse was needed. This came from Nicholas of Cusa (Nicolaus Cusanus). Nicholas was a cardinal, diplomat, mystic and scientist. He was one of the first to take empiricism, sensory perception, seriously. He said: If God is infinite, he cannot be outside Creation (nature and cosmos). God has no boundaries, so he can be found everywhere. Nicholas developed this notion by means of pure mathematical reasoning. In doing so, Nicholas questioned the prevailing medieval view of the world, in which God was outside Creation.

Shortly after Nicholas, Copernicus (1473–1543) confirmed this in a different way when he postulated that the sun was the centre of the universe and that everything orbited around it. Traditionally, people regarded the sun as the symbolic home of Jesus, so that Copernicus more or less placed Christ at the centre of the universe. This would have pleased Nicholas. To him, God was in all things:

> It is clear that God, who is the universe, is in all
> things and every existing thing is immediately
> in God, as is the case with the universe. Accord-
> ingly, to say that 'every thing is in every thing'
> means nothing but 'through all things God is in
> all things' and 'through all things all things are
> in God'.[121]

But we should not take this as meaning that God is all things. This would be a form of pantheism; that God corresponds to his Creation. God is *in* all things, but he does not correspond to all things. He remains the Other at the same time.

Through mathematical-philosophical reasoning, Nicholas of Cusa developed the notion that God is in all things. Copernicus developed more or less the same idea by investigating the firmament. However, a theological foundation was lacking. This was found when the *Corpus Hermeticum* was translated in Florence in 1460. In this work, people found what they sought: the cosmos was the Son of God, and mankind was the grandchild of God. The *Corpus Hermeticum* is a collection of hermetic writings from the second century. It is not Christian but heathen. This was not a problem to Renaissance man, because Hermes was mankind's first teacher. He was also the teacher of Plato and Moses. It is not true, of course, but that does not matter, as this was how he was regarded. Thus, Hermes enjoyed considerable status. He was soon incorporated into Christian thought, and this was the origin of hermetic Christianity, or Christian hermeticism, in which the cosmos/nature was animated by Christ Himself. Christ was active in nature. He was consistently engaged in transubstantiating nature, as it were. He was busy renewing the cosmos. People agreed with Paul in his hymn to Christ in which he says: He is the image of the invisible God, the first-born of all Creation; for in him all things were created ... all things were created through him and for him. (Col.1:15f). Christ, the Son of God, is active in Creation.

People in Christian hermeticism subscribd to these ideas. Paracelsus (1493–1541), Agrippa von Nettesheim (1486–1533), Valentin Wiegel (1533–88) all did so. Wiegel said that 'God is the being of all beings ... and nevertheless God is not Creation.'[122] This was the beginning of natural philosophy or radical pietism. They were genuine pietists. For example, Jakob Böhme wrote in one of his pious Christian documents:

> O God in Jesus Christ, who became a man for the
> poor sinner, please help them! I make my plea to
> you, for I have a spark of the refuge in my soul for
> you. I have not honoured your legacy, which we
> poor people have obtained by your bitter death,
> and share in Your Father's wrath with the legacy of
> vanity in the curse of the earth and am trapped in
> sin and half-dead in your empire. I lie impotently in
> your power and grim death awaits me.[123]

Calvin himself could not have said it better. Nevertheless, Böhme, like most natural philosophers, was also a scientist and alchemist. This was not so strange, because alchemy was the great art of transubstantiation of matter. Alchemists performed godly work. They helped Christ in the renewal of Creation. In his *Christianopolis,* another alchemist, Johann Valentin Andreae (1586–1654) — who also wrote the Rosicrucian documents in 1614–16 — stated the following:

> Just as we now regard the things in nature with
> veiled light, it will one day be the case that, when
> we have regained our ability to see due to the wood
> of the cross (Christ), we will not only see the sur-
> face but also the inside (of nature).[124]

By means of mystic investigation in Christ and in nature, people will one day be able to see Christ Himself in nature, through the exterior of the senses. Another natural philosopher, Christoph Friedrich Oetinger (1702–82), saw things this way when Newton (1642–1727) described gravity. Oetinger claimed that the effect of Christ was thus described. Gravity as the influence of Christ! Just like Andreae, Oetinger was a preacher as well as an alchemist and scientist; a combination that was not uncommon in those days.

Nonetheless, this was not so self-evident at the end of the eighteenth century. The Age of Enlightenment was then in full swing. In the Enlightenment, people did not seek knowledge of nature by means of mystic investigation but rather with the help of reason. According to the natural philosophers, you could not go much further than gaining knowledge of the 'surface.' To find Christ, it was necessary to develop higher (mystic) capabilities, and to find God it would take even more than that. The spiritual eye was needed, according to the natural philosophers. Enlightenment via the spiritual eye, or via reason, was the great discussion around 1800. Reason triumphed, as history has taught us. The alchemists and Rosicrucians were no longer the motivating scientific factor. This role was assumed by the natural sciences. There was little scope for esoteric Christianity. What remained was consigned to the background; it became clandestine. In was only in the Age of Enlightenment that the 'esoteric' gained the connotation of being 'secret.'

Esoteric Christianity in the twentieth century

Thanks to Helena Petrovna Blavatsky (see Chapter 6), the old alchemist and hermetic knowledge again came to the fore, against the materialist trend of the nineteenth century. Blavatsky could be called an esoteric, but she was not a Christian esoteric. Christianity did not interest her much. Her hermeticism was primarily a philosophical hermeticism. In the Theosophical Society, the members did not engage in practical hermeticism or alchemy. It was only Rudolf Steiner who began with such activities (see Chapter 6). From 1902 to 1913, Steiner was the chairman of the German Theosophical Society, but due to his Christina ideas, there was friction right from the outset. His views deviated considerably from those current in Theosophy, as we have seen. The Oriental leanings of Blavatsky became increasingly irritating to Steiner, who was seeking a Western-esoteric orientation. He found this in the irregular freemasons association entitled the Memphis and Misraïm Order (see Chapter 7). This variant of freemasonry was based on ancient Egyptian initiation. In accepting this, Steiner placed himself explicitly in the hermetic tradition. Steiner himself developed rites for this order.[125] A participant in Steiner's rituals summarized a lecture by Steiner on that topic as follows:

> The Misraïm cult was known in ancient Egypt and belonged to the most practised occult rituals in the mystery schools. We wish to perform these same rituals in our temple, but with the additions and reforms that Mark made. This Mark, to whom we are referring here, was a pupil of Peter, one of the twelve apostles, who wrote the Gospel According to Mark, and who stayed in Egypt as the Bishop of Alexandria. In conjunction with an Egyptian initiate, he reorganized the occult cult that we now know as the Misraïm cult.[126]

It is a charming occult fantasy from the *fin de siècle,* but that is not important. It is more important that people in the Memphis and Misraïm order felt linked to a Christianized Egyptian initiation practice.

Steiner developed a new initiation method that was related to the mystic tradition. His first series of public discourses as a follower of esotericism dealt with Western tradition.[127] Steiner allowed this tradition to begin with Jan van Ruusbroec, Meister Eckhart (1250–1327), Heinrich Suso (1295–1366) and Johannes Tauler (1300–1361), and went on to natural philosophy via Nicholas of Cusa, Paracelsus, and Agrippa von Nettesheim (1487–1535). Steiner referred to his initiations as 'spiritual natural laws.' This is a splendid description of the natural philosophical movement. Steiner describes his mystical path in *Knowledge of Higher Worlds.*[128] It is striking how closely this corresponds with the mystical path of Jan van Ruusbroec. But there is the essential difference that people did not use empiricism in the Middle Ages. So there was a form of 'spiritual knowledge' but not of 'spiritual natural laws.' Steiner regularly called the path of anthroposophical initiation a 'Rosicrucian path of initiation.' *Knowledge of Higher Worlds* was first published in 1904 and has been reprinted many times since then, with a supplementary foreword by Rudolf Steiner. Thus, Steiner taught his Rosicrucian initiation path in the time that he was chairman of the German Theosophical Society.

Steiner's Christian esotericism is not only philosophical, theosophical or theological in its nature, but also practical. Esotericism ought to lead to practical action and should not only be oriented to one's own initiation. This is the reason why anthroposophy has so-called 'working areas.' There is esotericism for education (Waldorf schools), esotericism for agriculture (bio-dynamic agriculture) and even for politics (social threefold order). The extent to which Steiner is actually following the tradition of natural philosophy is shown when one reads the texts of Agrippa von Nettesheim; for example, *Über die Fragwürdigkeit, ja Nichtigkeit der Wissenschaften, Künste und Gewerbe* (On the Dubious Nature, or the Insignificance of Science, Art and Design). In this document, Agrippa provides an overview of all the sciences of his day. It covers grammar, historiography, music, dance, the art of fighting, extracting metal, predicting the future, chiromancy ('reading' a face), natural philosophy, economics, agriculture, medicine, cooking, alchemy, law and prophetic theology. All facets of life are dealt with by Agrippa. And Steiner does the same.

With the renewal of all facets of life on the basis of an esoteric-Christian vision, Steiner distinguished himself and anthroposophy from the many new esoteric movements that evolved at that time.

Esoteric Christianity in modern times

At the beginning of the twentieth century, theosophy and anthroposophy were not the only new esoteric communities. A whole host of associations arose that all more or less derived from Theosophy. There were the Rosicrucian Fellowship, AMORC (Ancient Mystical Order of Rosi Crucis), and the Lectorum Rosicrucianum. All these communities or associations — along with modern freemasonry — were referred to as the New Religious Movements (NRMs), not to be confused with the New Age movement which arose at the end of the sixties. The difference is that the NRMs are organized and based on ancient initiation rituals, whereas the New Age movement is not organized in a society or association, and it is more oriented toward spiritual experience without the ballast of serious initiation practice and tradition. Where people in NRMs practise serious initiation rites to obtain insight into the spiritual world (and to become a better person), it seems that those in the New Age movement are seeking extra-sensory experiences without having to practise intensively.

At the same time, it also means that people in the New Age movement do not worry about theories and dogmas, which are prominent in the NRMs. After all, one does not join an

Anthroposophical Society or the Lectorium Rosicrucianum without reason. This is because one recognizes a communal element in the Anthroposophical Society or the Lectorium that is not present elsewhere. People in the New Age movement do not worry about these things. This means that the New Age movement is much more non-obligatory in its nature. One of the most important content-related differences is that NRMs are all more or less based on the Christian-hermetic tradition. This is the point of orientation. The orientation point in the New Age movement is having spiritual experiences. Where they come from and what they are related to is not very important, as long as one has spiritual experiences. This is a supplement to the esoteric tradition that could be of benefit to NRMs. And, vice versa, people in the New Age movement can take advantage of the initiation knowledge that is available in NRMs. This trend has actually gained momentum in the past decade. Fewer and fewer people feel the need to become a member of an NRM while an increasing number of New Age followers wish to attach themselves to some kind of tradition. People are growing toward one another, as it were.

This also offers new prospects for the Church and religion. To church-goers, the situation is as follows. Church-goers have to leave the Church if they go looking for more religious experience and perception, with the tragic consequence that church-goers are driven into the arms of the New Age movement, while they may not really wish to do so. This also applies to NRMs: being a member of an NRM also means that one has to leave the Church. Or an NRM has to have its own Church.

This idea of partitioning is slowly being abandoned, so that people can remain a member of the Church while simultaneously engaging in more esoteric matters. The 'vagueness' of the New Age movement and the Eastern tradition are decreasing. An increasing amount of New Age literature with Christian orientation is appearing, such as the *The Da Vinci Code*. This kind of book stimulates the thoughts of many church-goers, and simultaneously gets many New Age people interested in

Christianity. This process has been going on in smaller circles for some time, as shown by the New Age thinking of Hans Stolp and the books of Jacob Slavenburg. In the theological faculties, too, a change of attitude can also be perceived, albeit small and very gradual. Gnosticism is no longer exclusively dealt with from a heretical perspective, and increasing attention is being devoted to mystical tradition. These are excellent developments. They may be taking place much too slowly in the Church and in theology, but that is only logical. One must always take into account the struggle between the 'deviants' and the 'constants;' the progressives against the conservatives. This is also the case with the NRMs, which are undergoing the same kind of struggle. Perhaps this is a necessary step.

All these developments indicate that the spirit of the times is changing. Being engaged in esoteric matters is no longer a 'clandestine' activity, 'reserved for initiates.' People are engaged in esotericism throughout society. Interest in esoteric Christianity is growing rapidly. Perhaps partly due to Dan Brown.

Epilogue

The Da Vinci Code states that Jesus and Mary Magdalene were married and that they had a child called Sarah. This thought has become amazingly popular. A genuine tidal wave of books has flooded the market, elaborating on the marriage between Jesus and Mary Magdalene. Many believers find the idea of marriage an attractive one, because it brings Jesus closer to them. This is, of course, a fine thought. But the important questions are: Where did Dan Brown get his idea, and is there any truth in it?

Dan Brown based his idea primarily on two sources: the Gnostic texts *The Gospel of Mary Magdalene* and *The Gospel of Philip*. Both documents show that Jesus had a special relationship with Mary Magdalene, different from the one he had with the other apostles. Jesus loved her more than the other apostles and often kissed her on the mouth — at least, that is how Dan Brown quotes both texts. However, the *Gospel of Philip* does not state that Jesus kissed Mary Magdalene on her mouth. The relevant word in the original Nag Hammadi text is missing. This gives reason for doubt.

'Loving' and 'kissing' are typical words used in initiation. The *Gospel of Mary Magdalene* and the *Gospel of Philip* are initiation documents. The special relationship that Jesus had with Mary Magdalene is an initiation relationship. Mary Magdalene is simply more initiated than the other apostles. There is no mention of a physical marriage but rather of a marriage of initiation, a mystical union in which Christ is the bridegroom and Mary Magdalene the bride, as explained by mystics of all ages in the Song of Songs, which is regarded as a mystical document.

So *The Da Vinci Code* is not in the least a revelation of secrets that were kept hidden by the Church. It is a materialist explanation of a mystical marriage. The notion that Jesus was married to Mary Magdalene is pseudo-esotericism.

In this book I have elucidated the significance that many mystics have assigned to 'the kiss,' from the Church Father, Origen (185–254), to the Flemish female mystic, Hadewych (1210–1260), and on to the German mystic Jakob Böhme (1575–1624). In all cases, the mystic kiss is an expression of the *unio mystica* with Christ.

I have subsequently dealt with the widely dispersed idea that the Cathars, the Grail Knights and the Knights Templar were the keepers of the Holy Grail in the Middle Ages. According to Dan Brown, the Grail is the secret of the marriage and the child. I illustrated that the Cathars could have had nothing to do with the Grail. Medieval Grail literature shows that the Grail Knights meet the resurrected Christ when they find the Grail. In other words, the Grail literature deals with the crucifixion and the resurrection. This is not the case with the Cathars, who did not believe in the crucifixion and the resurrection. Their faith was based on Docetism. Grail literature arose among the practitioners of Cistercian mysticism, with the idea of civilizing the unruly medieval knights. When the Grail knight goes off on his quest, he must live a celibate life. Lancelot is not successful in this, and this is why he cannot find the Grail. The Grail and the Cathars make an uneasy combination. This also applied to the Templars. The regulations of the Order of the Templars were written by Bernard of Clairvaux (1090–1153), the founder of the order of the Cistercians and inaugurator of medieval mysticism. The Grail and the Templars were inter-related, but not the Templars and the Cathars.

The Templars also had to live celibately. There is no mention of a so-called *hiëros gamos* ritual — the ritual described by Dan Brown, in which the Templars achieved enlightenment due to sexual rites. In reports formulated by the Inquisition, the Templars were accused of sodomy but not of licentiousness with women. In addition, the confessions of the Templars were the result of torture, and the confessions were retracted immediately when they were sentenced. Dan Brown also erroneously mentioned that the Templars were persecuted by the Pope. However, this was the work of the French king. The Pope attempted to save what he could. After all, the Templars were his militia. The Templars were not followers of esotericism.

Dan Brown says that he wishes to place the woman, as well as sexual union between man and woman, on the pedestal where it belongs. He claims that the Church has always regarded the women and sex in a poor light. I have modified this view. Since the beginning of the Christian era, the entire Western culture has had a negative approach to women. The Church is a component of Western culture, so it is logical that the Church has an anti-feminine attitude. However, one can also maintain that the Church has been the one organization that has tried to stand up for women. The Blessed Mary is still the Mother of God, right up to the present day. And Mary Magdalene is the example, *par excellence,* of a perfect convert. She has always been seen this way, and copied down through the ages. Of course, there have been excesses but not only excesses.

The fact that the Church has always regarded sex as a negative phenomenon is not particularly interesting. It is much more interesting to examine why. I have developed an appealing theory. In the pre-Christian mysteries, sex, in general, was supervised by temple priests and priestesses. The virgin birth of Jesus expresses the idea that Mary was free of lust. The apocryphal gospels indicate that the marriage between Joseph and Mary was sealed under the supervision of the temple and that Mary was a temple virgin. However, around the beginning of the Christian era, the mysteries began to decline and became decadent. One only needs to look as the Roman Emperors to see this trend. Sex was regarded as an unbridled urge; the *motus inordinatus,* which Augustine complained about, and which troubled him greatly in his younger years. It pulled a person downwards rather than elevating him or her. For this reason, the Church attempted to limit it; God-seekers and priests had to live celibately, and sex between man and women was only for the purpose of procreation. The young Church must have thought that people were not able to cope with 'free sex.' It may be the case that the Church has sheltered us from an orgy of sexual desire for two thousand years. That is no longer needed; we are now capable of controlling our *motus inordinatus* ourselves, in contrast to what many television programmes propagate.

Finally, I dealt with the idea that the rabbis in ancient Jewish times were all married, so that Jesus would also have been married. He is addressed as 'rabbi' (master or teacher) in the New Testament. Nevertheless, there are examples in the Talmud of rabbis who were celibate, and that was certainly the case in various esoteric sects in the time of Jesus. The Essenes — to which Jesus allegedly belonged for some time — had celibate priests. John the Baptist was certainly celibate. He was the prophet of a certain baptismal sect in Jewry, who were known for their celibate priests. Jesus was baptized by him, so it is quite logical that he would also be celibate.

There is nothing wrong with the fact that *The Da Vinci Code* is based on quicksand. The book stimulates thought on this serious topic, and interest in the life of Jesus is increasing, *nolens volens*. However, the fact that pseudo-esotericism is taking place is not a good development. Dan Brown turns Jesus Christ into a 'normal person,' as has been the case in theology for the past 150 years. However, I defend the traditional idea of the dual-nature theory: Jesus is both man and God. Being able to accept this is true esotericism.

Notes

1. See, among others, H. Stolp, *Jezus mijn broeder* (Jesus My Brother), Deventer 2005.
   J. Slavenburg, *De logische Jezus* (The Logical Jesus), Deventer 1999.
   J. Slavenburg, *Valsheid in geschrifte,* (Forged Documents), Deventer 1996 (4). In this book, Slavenburg states that the marriage at Cana may have been that of Jesus and Mary Magdalene.
2. See www.revelations.com and K. & C. van Huffelen, *Maria Magdalena en de (Schijn) Heiligen. De waarheid achter De Da Vinci Code* (Mary Magdalene and the Sanctimonious. The truth behind the Da Vinci Code), Barchem 2006.
3. *Gospel of Mary,* BC, 10.
4. *Gospel of Mary,* BC, 18.
5. D. Brown, *The Da Vinci Code.*
6. D. Brown, *The Da Vinci Code.*
7. *The Gospel According to Philip,* NHC, II, 3 (55).
8. *The Nag Hammadi Library,* ed. J.M. Robinson, Leiden/ New York/Copenhagen/ Cologne 1988.
9. *Cologne Mani Codex* (135).
10. *Verhandeling over de achtse en negende Hemelsfeer* (Treatise on the Eighth and Ninth Heavenly Sphere), NHC, VI, 6 (52).
11. *Verhandeling* (57).
12. *Asclepius,* 41b, transl. G. Quispel, Amsterdam 1996.
13. H.J. Polotsky and A. Böhlig, *Kephalaia,* IX, p.37, Manichäische Handschriften der Staatlichen Museen Berlin, Stuttgart 1940.
14. *Kephalaia,* IX, p.38, line 22–33, p.39, 1.24–30.
15. *Psalmen des Herrn Herakleides.*
16. H. Stolp, *Jezus mijn Broeder* (Jesus My Brother), Deventer 2005, pp.92–93.
17. *Revelation of Peter,* NHC, VII, 3 (71).
18. *Revelation of Peter* (81).
19. *(First) Revelation of James,* NHC, V, 3 (31).
20. *(First) Revelation of James,* (24).
21. Origen, *Hom, in Cant. I,* GCS 33 (1925).

22. Eusebius, *Historiae ecclesiasticus,* VI, 1, 11–12.
23. Justinus Martyr, *Apologia* I, LXV.
24. Tertullian, *De Praescriptone Haereticorum,* 41.
25. Bernard of Clairvaux, *Sermones Super Cantica Canticorum,* II, 2.
26. Bernard of Clairvaux, *Sermones Super Cantica Canticorum,* III, 1.
27. Hadewych, *Visionen* (Visions), VII.
28. Hadewych, *Visionen* (Visions), VII.
29. Teresa of Avila, *Castilio interior,* VII, iii, 13.
30. Jodocus van Lodenstein, *Preek over Hooglied* (Sermon on the Song of Songs), 1:4.
31. J. Böhme, *Der Weg zu Christo* (The Path to Christ), Book I, 32.
32. J. Böhme, *Der Weg zu Christo* (The Path to Christ), Book I, 38.
33. J. Böhme, *Der Weg zu Christo* (The Path to Christ), Book I, 47.
34. See *The Chymical Wedding of Christian Rosencreutz.*
35. *Gospel According to Philip* (44), translation by Paterson Brown.
36. *Gospel According to Philip* (86), translation by Paterson Brown.
37. *Gospel According to Philip* (80), translation by Paterson Brown.
38. *Gospel According to Philip* (86), translation by Paterson Brown.
39. *Gospel According to Philip* (108), translation by Paterson Brown.
40. *Gospel According to Philip* (119), translation by Paterson Brown.
41. *Gospel According to Mary Magdalene* (9:1).
42. *Gospel According to Philip* (21).
43. *Gospel of Nicodemus* (15:6), transl. M.R. James
44. Robert de Boron, *L'Estoire dou Graal.*
45. *L'Estoire dou Graal.*
46. *L'Estoire dou Graal.*
47. W. Map, *Queste del Saint Graal,* trans. M. Matarasso, *The Quest of the Holy Grail,* London 1969 p.275.
48. *Queste del Saint Graal.*
49. W. Malmesbury, *De Regum Gestis Anglorum,* in R. White (ed.), *King Arthur in Legend and History,* London 1997, p.22.
50. See R.S. Loomis, *The Grail. From Celtic Myth to Christian Symbol,* Cardiff/New York, 1963, pp.178f.
51. G. Hilledal and B. Gustafsson, *De såg och hörde Jesus* (They Saw and Heard Jesus), Stockholm, Verbum.
52. H.W. Schroeder, *Von der Wiederkunft Christi heute* (On the Second Coming of Christ), Stuttgart 1999, p.93.

53. Wolfram von Eschenbach, *Parzival,* verse 462.

54. *Parzival,* verse 464.

55. *Parzival,* verse 448.

56. A. Gadal, *Sur le chemin du Saint Graal. Les anciens mystères Cathares* (The Path to the Holy Grail. The ancient Catharian mysteries).

57. Inquistion register of Jacques Fournier. Latin manuscript No.4030.

58. *Ibid.*

59. *Ibid.*

60. H.M. Kuitert, *Het algemeen betwijfeld christelijk geloof. Een herziening* (The generally doubted Christian faith. A review), Kampen 1992, p.138.

61. *Gnostic Apocalypse of Peter,* transl. Jackson Snyder.

62. See H. Spencer Lewis, *The Mystical Life of Jesus.*

63. See H.J. Spierenburg, *The New Testament Commentaries of H.P. Blavatsky,* San Diego 1987.

64. H.J. Spierenburg (comp.), *The Inner Group Teachings of H.P. Blavatsky to her Personal Pupils (1890–91),* San Diego.

65. Brown, *The Da Vinci Code,* Ch.55.

66. Tom Harpur, *The Pagan Christ — Recovering the Lost Light,* Thomas Allen, Toronto 2004.

67. Harpur, pp.82f.

68. Harpur, pp.143f.

69. E. Renan, *La vie de Jésus* (The Life of Jesus), Paris 1863, Chapter IV.

70. See H.M. Kuitert, *Jesus, nalatenschap van het christendom* (Jesus, legacy of Christianity), Kampen 1998.

71. R. Steiner, *Aus der Akasha-Forschung. Das Fünfte Evangelium* (GA 148). Translated in *The Fifth Gospel,* Rudolf Steiner Press, London 1968. Lecture of Oct 3, 1913.

72. R. Steiner, *Die dreifache Sonne und der auferstandene Christus* (GA 211), lecture April 24, 1922.

73. The Wisdom of Solomon is part of the Apocryphal Old Testament.

74. Minucius Felix, *Octavius,* VIII, 3–9, 5.

75. Epiphanius, *Panarion,* 26, 5, 2–6 GCS 24.

76. Augustine, *De Haeresibus,* XLVI, CCL 46.

77. *Adamari Historianum libri* III, 59 MGH. SS, IV. Transl. W.L. Wakefield and A.P. Evans, *Heresies of the High Middle Ages. Selected Sources. Translated and Annotated,* New York/London 1969, p.75.

78. Guiberti Abbatis, *De vita sua, libra tres,* III PL 156. Transl. Wakefield and Evans, p.103.

79. *De nugis curialium,* i.xxx, ed. Montague R. James, transl. Wakefield and Evans, pp.252–53.

80. Bernard of Clairvaux, *De laude novae militae.*

81. *Lettres des premiers Chartreux,* SC 88, 1988.

82. G. Lizerdand, *Le dossier de l'affair des Templiers,* 1923.

83. Abbreviated text of A. Crowley, *Oefenboek voor Astraal en Symboolmagie* (Exercise Book for Astral and Symbol Magic), collection of lectures, Amsterdam 1987, p.120.

84. Crowley, pp.180f.

85. Augustine, *De civitate Dei,* XXII, II.

86. *De civitate Dei,* III, 5.

87. Apuleius, *The Golden Ass,* book XI.

88. *The Nativity of Mary* 7:4.

89. See J.L.M van Schaik, *Unde Malum. Dualisme van manicheeers en catharen,* Kampen 2004.

90. *De civitate Dei,* XIII, 13, p.597.

91. Minucius Felix, *Octavius,* VIII, 3–9, 5.

92. *Vita Antoni.*

93. Map, *Queste,* pp.112f.

94. Robert de Boron, *Vita Merlini.*

95. Dante Alighieri, *Divinia Comedia,* Inferno, canto 5.

96. Abelarde, *Historia Calamitatum mearum,* VII, 5.

97. Abelarde, *Historia.*

98. St Jerome, *Epistulae,* 22.

99. Hildegard of Bingen, *Briefwechsel, dritter Brief an Kaiser Friedrich* (Correspondence, third letter to Emperor Frederick).

100. *Epistolario di Caterina de Siena,* D.I. I, vi, Rome, 1940.

101. Bernard of Clairvaux, *In laudibus Verginis Matris.*

102. Bernard of Clairvaux, *Sermones Super Cantica Canticorum,* 57, II.

103. Thomas à Kempis, *Imitatio Christi,* II, viii.

104. Kempis, IV, xi.

105. A. Bake, *Mijn Beghin ende voortghank.*

106. Calvin, *Institution,* III, 20,22.

107. U. Zwingli, *Sixty-Seven Articles,* article xix.
108. Second Vatican Council, *Lumen Gentium,* Ch.8.
109. See, for example, E.A. de Boer, *Maria Magdalena. De Mythe Voorbij (*Mary Magdalene). Beyond the Myth), Zoetermeer 2005.
110. Abreviated version of the text in G.R.S. Mead, *Gnostic John the Baptizer: Selections from the Mandaean John-Book,* 1924, section 9.
111. Flavius Josephus, *De Bello Judaico* (Jewish Wars) II. See also Flavius Josephus, *Antiquitates Judaicae (Antiquities of the Jews),* XVIII, 18.
112. Babylonian Talmud, *'Hagigah,* 14b.
113. Tosefta, *Yebamoth* 8.7.
114. Valentinus, *The Gospel of Truth,* 9,10.
115. *Pistis Sophia,* trans G.S.R. Mead, ch.1.
116. Augustine, *De Civitate Dei,* XI, 4.
117. Augustine, *Confessions,* 4.12.18.
118. Hadewych, *Letters,* XVIII.
119. J. van Ruusbroec, *Van den XII Beghinen* (Of the XII Beguines).
120. B. Silvestris, *Cosmographia,* II, iv.
121. N. Cusanus, *De docta Ignnoranntia,* II, ix, 118 (trans. H.L. Bond, *Nicholas of Cusa. Selected Spiritual Writings,* New York 1997.
122. V. Wiegel, *Informatorium oder kurzer Unterricht* (Information or Brief Education), collected writings), 3 Lieferung. P.1118.
123. J. Böhme, *Der Weg zu Christo* (The Path to Christ).
124. J.V. Andreae, *Christianopolis.*
125. *From the History and Contents of the First Section of the Esoteric School 1904–1914,* Anthroposophic Press, Hudson 1998.
   Concerning the History and Content of the Higher Degrees of the Esoteric School 1904–1914, Etheric Dimensions Press, Switzerland & Scotland 2005.
126. R. Steiner, *Zur Geschichte und aus den Inhalten der erkenntniskultischen Abteilung der Esoterischen Schule 1904–1914,* (GA 265), see *Concerning the History* (note 125 above).
127. *Mystics After Modernism, Discovering the Seeds of a New Science in the Renaissance,* Anthroposophic Press, Hudson 2000.
128. *Knowledge of Higher Worlds, How is it Achieved?* Rudolf Steiner Press, Forest Row 2004. Also publishes as *How to Know Higher Worlds, A Modern Path of Initiation,* Anthroposophic Press, Hudson 1994.

Index